WITHDRAWN

DOCUMENTARY
STUDIES IN
MODERN RUSSIAN
POETRY   Memoirs, biographies,
and critical views, in newly translated
editions, by and about the exceptional
men and women of the early
twentieth-century renascence
in Russian poetry.

GENERAL EDITORS: Robert P. Hughes
AND Simon Karlinsky

1.   *The Diary of Valery Bryusov (1893–1905).*
      With Reminiscences by V. F. Khodasevich and
      Marina Tsvetaeva. Edited, Translated, and
      with an Introductory Essay by Joan Delaney
      Grossman. 1980.

2.   Vladimir Zlobin. *A Difficult Soul: Zinaida*
      Gippius. Edited, Annotated, and with an In-
      troductory Essay by Simon Karlinsky. 1980.

3.   Andrei Bely. *Reminiscences of Alexander Blok.*
      Translated, Annotated, and with an Introduc-
      tory Essay by Robert P. Hughes. 1981.

A Difficult Soul

Zinaida Gippius. Watercolor by Leon Bakst, 1905.

VLADIMIR ZLOBIN

A Difficult Soul:
Zinaida Gippius

EDITED, ANNOTATED,
AND WITH AN
INTRODUCTORY ESSAY
BY Simon Karlinsky

University of California Press

BERKELEY · LOS ANGELES · LONDON

University of California Press
Berkeley and Los Angeles, California
University of California Press, Ltd.
London, England
Copyright © 1980 by
The Regents of the University of California
Printed in the United States of America

1 2 3 4 5 6 7 8 9

Library of Congress Cataloging in Publication Data

Zlobin, Vladimir.
  A difficult soul.

  (Documentary studies in modern Russian poetry)
  Translation of Tiazhelaia dusha.
  Includes index.
  1. Gippius, Zinaida Nikolaevna, 1869–1945.
2. Poets—Russian—20th century—Biography.
I. Karlinsky, Simon. II. Title. III. Series.
PG3460.G5Z9813   891.71′3 [B]   78-66043
ISBN 0-520-03867-3

Contents

81-1196

Who Was Zinaida Gippius?

The miraculously rich period in Russian poetry which began in the 1890s and had its maximal flowering in the first three decades of the twentieth century came to its unarguable end with the death of Anna Akhmatova in 1966. As that period recedes into history and as its complexity can gradually be grasped and understood as a coherent literary pattern, it becomes evident that the main trends and achievements of that age can be epitomized—though certainly not exhaustively—by the three women poets whose work typified the three principal poetic schools of their time. Zinaida Gippius (1869–1945) was one of the main initiators of the poetic renascence known as Russian Symbolism, the originator of the verse forms and thematic concerns that helped shape the poetics of Alexander Blok, Andrei Bely, and numerous other poets. Anna Akhmatova (1889–1966) was central to the sober-minded, neo-realistic poetics of Acmeism. Marina Tsvetaeva (1892–1941), who never joined a literary school in her life and would have bristled at being termed a Futurist poet, nevertheless summarized in her work all that was finest in the lexically and structurally innovative literary art of the Russian Futurists.

As a poet, Zinaida Gippius is the equal of these two great younger contemporaries. As a historical phenomenon, she is probably more important than either of them. One of the guiding spirits of the entire Symbolist movement, and a pioneer of the turn-of-the-century religious revival among the liberal intelligentsia, a revival that had incalculable consequences for twentieth-century Russian culture, Gippius was also a remarkable early theoretician and practitioner of androgyny and psychological unisex, who rejected the traditional male/female roles as early as the 1890s.

In any other country, the value of her achievement as a poet, the originality of her social, sexual, and religious views, and the impact of these views on the intellectual trends of her time would have by now resulted in a wide array of critical and biographical studies of Gippius, assessing her significance and influence. But her violently anti-Bolshevik stance after the Revolution made her an un-person in the Soviet Union in post-revolutionary times, while her religious and political radicalism did not sit well with the growing conservatism of both Soviet and émigré literary scholarship from the 1930s on. In recent times, Gippius has been studied by a few Western scholars who publish their work in English, most notably Temira Pachmuss and Olga Matich. The only book about her to have so far appeared in Russian is *A Difficult Soul* (*Tyazhelaya dusha*) by her long-time secretary and factotum, Vladimir Zlobin, printed in Madrid and published in Washington, D.C., in 1970 and offered here in an English translation.

Although possessing some trappings of a biography and containing much indispensable biographical information, Zlobin's book is primarily a study of the poet's relationships with the two beings who were, after her husband Dmitry Merezhkovsky, the principal *dramatis personae* of her life: the critic Dmitry Filosofov and the Devil. As Zlobin points out, Gippius believed in the corporeal existence of the Devil, just as Gogol and Dostoevsky did earlier. The reality of her struggle with the Devil and the parallel reality of her *amour impossible* for the unattainable Dmitry Filosofov constitute the high drama of Zlobin's book.

Vladimir Zlobin undoubtedly knew Gippius through a long and close association, and yet some of his book's central insights come from the memoir on Gippius by the poet and publisher Sergei Makovsky, which was included in his book *On the Parnassus of the Silver Age* (*Na Parnase Serebrianogo veka* [Munich, 1962]). It was while Makovsky helped Zlobin sort out the literary archive of Gippius and Merezhkovsky (Zlobin was their heir and executor) that Makovsky and, after him, Zlobin were able to formulate the sexual and religious modalities that were at the basis of both the life and the poetry of Zinaida Gippius.

Zlobin shared the lives of Gippius and Merezhkovsky for more than a quarter of a century. He was physically present at many of the scenes he describes. Yet throughout the book, he chooses not to mention himself or his participation in the events. Admirable as this reticence may seem, it also results in a slightly blurred, out-of-focus perspective in some of the book's passages. The fact that Zlobin had to rely on Makovsky to perceive the central theme of his book suggests that he himself was too close to the book's protagonists, both physically and emotionally, to attain the minimal distance necessary for an overall, coherent view. *A Difficult Soul* is consequently a highly personal book, idiosyncratic, and at times digressive. Zlobin's historical outlook can also be hazy on occasion, as in his ascribing the gift of political prophesy to Gippius in chapter six, a point that is based on Zlobin's confusion of the Bolsheviks with the Russian Social

Democrats, of which the Bolsheviks were but one faction. With all that, his strategic position in the Merezhkovsky circle provided Zlobin with the kind of insights into the mind and the poetry of Zinaida Gippius that make his book in many ways our best key to understanding her.

2

For a poet and thinker of such complexity, the formative influences on Gippius were surprisingly few. The essential ones were her reading of Dostoevsky at an early age and, as Zlobin suggests, an equally early exposure to Lermontov's narrative poem "The Demon." Her enthusiasm for Dostoevsky determined her subsequent literary tastes and sympathies, causing her later hostility to almost all the twentieth-century literary figures who were not in some way descended from the Dostoevskian tradition. In the 1890s she was influenced, in a rather general way, by the foreign thinkers who were basic to the formation of Russian Symbolism, most notably Schopenhauer, Nietzsche, and Ibsen. Like most other Symbolists, she fell under the spell of the idealistic and mystical teachings of Vladimir Solovyov. Apart from this, Gippius seems to have arrived at her theology, philosophy, and poetics on her own or in collaboration with Merezhkovsky.

Gippius and Merezhkovsky were married in 1889, when she was nineteen. They lived together, inseparably, for the rest of their lives, in a fraternal, apparently never-consummated marriage which was an intellectual partnership more than anything else. Zlobin insists that the generative or fertilizing role in this relationship belonged to Gippius. He might well be right as far as Merezhkovsky's celebrated trilogy of historical novels is concerned (*Julian the Apostate, The Romance of Leonardo da Vinci*, which served Sigmund Freud as a primary source for his psychoanalysis of Leonardo, and *Peter and Alexis*) and even more so with regard to his later novel *Birth of the Gods*, with its remarkable insights into sexual variants and sex role ambiguities. Yet, while Zinaida Gippius was a major poet, which Merezhkovsky, for all the voluminous verse he published throughout his life, was not, and while she was in most other areas the more original thinker of the two, Merezhkovsky was her superior in the field of literary criticism. His studies of Tolstoy, Dostoevsky, and especially Gogol laid the foundation of twentieth-century understanding of these major writers, putting an end (at least in pre-Soviet times) to the simplistic, utilitarian reading of their work as mere topical social commentary, and helping to establish the full scope and complexity of their individual achievements.

Both Gippius and Merezhkovsky published their earliest poetry in the 1880s. It was a time when several decades of domination over literature by dogmatic, utilitarian-minded, radical critics, who tolerated poetry only when it preached elementary morality or contained social criticism, had brought poetic taste and understanding to its lowest point in modern Russian history. The decade of the eighties was dominated by the maudlin poetaster Semyon Nadson, acclaimed as a new incarnation of Pushkin merely because he wrote mainly of the evils of oppression and tyranny. Merezhkovsky's poetry never quite managed to shake off all traces of Nadsonism, but Gippius liberated herself from it, quickly and triumphantly. The poems she wrote in 1893 and 1894, initially rejected by some of the best literary journals of the time, marked the beginning of modern Russian poetry. In her verse of those years, Gippius expanded the boundaries of traditional Russian metrics, popularized the use of accentual verse (previously found in a few exceptional poems by such earlier figures as Vasily Zhukovsky and Afanasy Fet) and initiated the use of assonance rhymes. All these features were later developed and perfected by other important twentieth-century poets, among them Blok, Akhmatova, and Osip Mandelstam. But Gippius led the way. Without her pioneering example, neither Alexander Blok nor Vladimir Mayakovsky could have been what they later became.

Equally essential for the development of twentieth-century poetry in Russia were the themes of her poetry of the early 1890s. Some of her poems addressed themselves to social topics, but Gippius was primarily a philosophical and religious poet, possibly Russia's most profound religious poet of all time. She was one of the first to take up in her poetry the themes that were to become the central ones of much of Russian Symbolism as a whole: humanity's need for religious faith, the problem of achieving freedom in a necessity-bound world, the ambiguities of sex roles in most love relationships, the evil forces present in this world, and the inevitability of death as an ever-present factor in our lives. It is not an exaggeration to say that Gippius confronted in her poetry many of the basic themes that Dostoevsky treated in his novels and gave them her own original solutions or that, in a sense, she occupies in Russian poetry the position that Dostoevsky occupies in the Russian novel.

3

     In almost all her poems, Gippius speaks of herself in the masculine gender (much more fully expressed in Russian grammar than in English). In her love lyrics, this masculine persona frequently addresses a female love object. The same ambivalence was also present in her personal life. Her intellectual partnership with Merezhkovsky remained the most important of her relationships, but it failed to satisfy all of her emotional needs. Her diary *Contes d'amour: A Diary of My Love Affairs,* which was published by Professor Temira Pachmuss in the Russian émigré journal *Vozrozhdenie* (*La Renaissance*),[1] tells of her adolescent infatuations with young schoolboys prior to her marriage and of her emotional involvements with a number of leading intellectuals of the period, including the critic Akim Volynsky and the poet and playwright Nikolai Minsky (the author of the remarkable pro-feminist drama *Alma*) during the first ten years of her marital life. In all of these relationships, Gippius was the initiator, with the men following her lead and complying with her wishes. In love with the idea of love, starved for a sensual outlet, she repeatedly broke off these affairs after a few inconclusive confessions and kisses, all too clearly unable or unwilling to assume the traditional female role.

    Sergei Makovsky recalls that at the age of thirty Gippius affected a peasant-style hairdo that involved a braid

1. Numbers 211 and 212 (1969). A censored and abridged version in English is to be found in *Between Paris and St. Petersburg: Selected Diaries of Zinaida Gippius*, ed. Temira Pachmuss (Urbana: University of Illinois Press, 1975).

wound around her head and was intended to proclaim her unsullied virginity after ten years of married life. "A most telling detail," Makovsky adds. "Who but Gippius would have thought of flaunting so immodestly the 'purity' of her conjugal life, which took such an unusual form in her case." Like several other memoirists, Makovsky hints that Gippius was physically a hermaphrodite and was biologically incapable of engaging in heterosexual relations. What is significant in literary terms is that the enormous burden of frustration which her need for love and the impossibility of consummation imposed on Gippius was powerfully expressed in her poetry.

In 1899 Gippius and Merezhkovsky spent the summer in the Sicilian town of Taormina in close association with the male homosexual coterie around Baron Wilhelm von Gloeden, the pioneering photographer of male nudes, whose work has been rediscovered and revived in the two recent books devoted to his art. "On the Shores of the Ionian Sea," a travelogue by Gippius which was serialized in Sergei Diaghilev's journal *The World of Art* in 1899, contains her account of her association with von Gloeden, complete with a discrete description of an all-male dance she attended at his studio. Gippius was fascinated and perturbed by the possibilities revealed to her by the von Gloeden circle. She was repelled by what she called the "extreme specialization" of the male homosexuals she met, considering it every bit as unacceptable to her as the exclusive heterosexuality of men "for whom other men do not exist." Yet she was enormously attracted by the spiritual and emotional aspects of love between men: "It is equally good and natural for any person to love any other person. Love between men *may be* boundlessly beautiful and God-given, like any other love." In the same entry in *Contes d'amour* (August 16, 1899), Gippius admitted that she found homosexuals physically more attractive than other men: "What appeals to me in all this is the illusion of a possibility, a kind of hint at bisexuality, so that he seems to be both a woman and a man. This is terribly close to what I need."

While she was charmed by the emotional perspectives that same-sex love opened up for her, she assumed a disdainful attitude to the physical consummation of this love. Both she and Merezhkovsky took very seriously the ideas, current at the end of the nineteenth century, that homosexuality was the result of degeneration and that physical sex between males was ruinous to their health. Merezhkovsky, who wrote of lesbian love with sympathy and understanding in *Birth of the Gods*, drew a sharp distinction in his historical and philosophical treatise *Secret of the West: Europe-Atlantis* (1930) between the androgynous men described by Plato, who experience a spiritual love for other males, and the "Sodomites" described in the novels of Marcel Proust, who give this love a physical expression and whose emergence presaged for Merezhkovsky the approaching collapse of Western civilization.

At the turn of the century, Anton Chekhov and after him the Symbolists, most notably Minsky, Merezhkovsky, and Sologub, inaugurated in Russian literature a new freedom in treating sexual topics. In matters of same-sex love, however, those years before Freud and Havelock Ellis (to say nothing of Kinsey) were still the Dark Ages. Vasily Rozanov, a close friend and frequent literary associate of both Gippius and Merezhkovsky, could publish in 1913 his book *People of Lunar Light*, which was on the one hand an eloquent defense of homosexuality as a valid alternative way of life, yet on the other hand asserted that true male homosexuals and lesbians have no interest in giving their form of love any sort of physical expression. This confusion and ignorance forms a background against which we can best understand the emotional predicament of Zinaida Gippius. A poet whose religious consciousness was the central fact of her existence, with sexual love an inalienable component and a natural mode of expressing this consciousness, she, paradoxically, had no clue about her own sexual identity.

Even today, when we have numerous terms to describe such things, it is hard to find the exact one that would fit her unique case. She was certainly not a bisexual, nor was she, despite an occasional infatuation with other women and a few love poems addressed to them, a lesbian. She was not a "man trapped in a woman's body," as some of today's transsexuals describe themselves. The closest term is the one that existed in her day: she was an androgyne. Primarily, though apparently not totally female physically, she felt herself to be a male intellectually and spiritually. Her ideal soul mate would have been a male androgyne, with a mirrorlike reversal of her traits. It was the tragic mistake of her life that she chose to settle for loving a male homosexual, whom she mistook for her true counterpart.

4

During her Taormina summer of 1899, Gippius came close to falling in love with a young Frenchman from Baron von Gloeden's entourage. He is mentioned in *Contes d'amour* under the name Briquet and is described as tall and slender, with "incredibly blue eyes," "very, very handsome," about twenty-four years old, "faultlessly elegant," and just a bit on the effeminate side. Despite his charm and considerable culture, Gippius mastered the emotions that Briquet seemed about to arouse in her, partly because he was what she called a "specialized" homosexual and partly because she felt that he was "externally and internally only a very close caricature of a being which, had it existed, could please me totally." That "being" turned out to be a young Russian, whom her description of Briquet also fitted in almost every particular—age, appearance, and personality—but who in addition spoke her language, was a man of letters, and could appreciate her intellect and literary achievement. Gippius had briefly met Dmitry Filosofov several years earlier, but it was only after her Taormina experiences that she understood how and why she wanted him and began her campaign to conquer him.

Dmitry Vladimirovich Filosofov (1872–1940) had an interesting family background. His father was a public prosecutor, whose career advancement was seriously handicapped by the pro-revolutionary sympathies and activities of his wife. Anna Pavlovna Filosofova, née Diaghileva (she was Sergei Diaghilev's aunt), was a prominent feminist of her time, highly active in political and literary life. Her ideological differences with her ultra-conservative husband did not prevent them from bringing five children into the world or from providing these children with a warm domestic atmosphere, as reflected in the memoirs of the famed painter and stage designer Alexander Benois, who was the classmate of the family's youngest son Dmitry at the May Gymnasium in St. Petersburg.

The school environment of Dmitry (usually called Dima) Filosofov has been described in several memoirs and is now studied by an ever-growing number of art historians, because that circle of bright and inquisitive boys was the nucleus of the most influential phenomenon in the artistic life of turn-of-the-century Russia, "The World of Art." It was their association of that name, which continued after they had left school and culminated in the publication of the journal of the same name, founded and edited by Filosofov and his cousin and lover Sergei Diaghilev, that was instrumental in bringing Russian art and literature out of the provincial isolation and stagnation of the last decades of the nineteenth century and into the dazzling artistic renascence of the early twentieth. Within the association, heterosexuals, such as Alexander Benois and Leon Bakst, coexisted and collaborated amicably with group members who were exclusively homosexual. Among the latter were the painter Konstantin Somov (who according to Benois had a passionate love affair with Filosofov while they were still at school) and the dilettante musician Walter Nouvel, Filosofov's lifelong friend, who later assisted Diaghilev in his ballet enterprises and who, according to the diaries of Gippius, carried a torch for the handsome Dima for the rest of his life.

The foundation of the journal *The World of Art* coincided with the return of Gippius and Merezhkovsky from Taormina. Along with the other important figures of the nascent Symbolist movement, they immediately became the journal's regular contributors. Since Filosofov was the literary editor of the journal, they dealt primarily with him, rather than with Diaghilev. With Merezhkovsky's willing assistance, Gippius soon set out to break up the relationship between Filosofov and Diaghilev, using as her main lever Filosofov's religious and mystical inclinations and interests, which Diaghilev was unable to share. By 1900 Filosofov had taken part in a series of secret discussions with the Merezhkovskys and some of their close friends, such as Nouvel and Nikolai Berdyaev, about the possibility of founding a private church, which was to supersede the Russian Orthodox one. In her journal *Of That Which Was* (*O byvshem*), Gippius noted that the perceptive Walter Nouvel suggested to her that "it might be that you are searching not for God, but for Filosofov, because you are personally attracted to him" and warned her that "should Filosofov realize that you are in love with him, he will certainly lose all interest in you and in your cause."

On Christmas Eve of 1901 (by the Western calendar), Gippius, Merezhkovsky, and Filosofov went through a mystical ceremony, part communion and part wedding, that symbolized their joint dedication to each other and to the future church they hoped to organize. Then Filosofov returned to Diaghilev and went with him on a trip to Italy. Yet within the same year he joined Gippius and Merezhkovsky in editing their new religious journal *The New Way*, which drew away many of the leading contributors to *The World of Art*, dissatisfied with Diaghilev's purely aesthetic stance. The result was a management crisis at *The World of Art*, which Diaghilev sought to solve by enlisting the editorial assistance of

Anton Chekhov. This crisis also found its expression in an impassioned polemic between Alexander Benois and Merezhkovsky, in the pages of *The New Way*, about the relationship of art to religion.

The tug-of-war between Gippius and Diaghilev over Filosofov's affections culminated in the victory of Gippius. In 1904 *The World of Art* ran into financial difficulties and ceased publication. Its function and its mission were taken over by a series of other splendid journals such as *The Balance, The Golden Fleece*, and *Apollo*. To the outside world, Gippius, Merezhkovsky, and Filosofov became a triumvirate, living together much of the time. They collaborated on the anti-monarchist tract *The Tsar and the Revolution*, banned in Russia and published in France and Germany, and they jointly wrote a remarkable and impressive play *Poppy Blossoms (Makov tsvet)*, a picture of the generational conflict occasioned by the 1905 revolution and aggravated by the polarization of opinion over the desirability and ethics of the Russo-Japanese War of 1904–1906.

Vladimir Zlobin's book shows some of the inner workings of this triumvirate. Gippius may have convinced Filosofov that his earlier "specialized" homosexuality was wrong for him, but there was no way for her to convert him into the androgynous being she wanted him to be or to make him respond physically to her passion. A complicating factor on which Zlobin does not dwell was Filosofov's apparent infatuation with the asexual Merezhkovsky, who was not able to reciprocate except on a purely spiritual plane. Zlobin's occasional animosity toward Gippius while describing her relationship to Filosofov can be explained by her lack of sympathy for Zlobin's own homosexuality.

5

The ostensibly private imbroglio among Gippius, Filosofov, and Diaghilev had an effect on the entire future of Russian culture which is not generally realized and which had ramifications going far beyond this highly special emotional tangle. Partly in order to keep Filosofov more securely within their orbit, Gippius and Merezhkovsky organized the famous series of encounters between the intellectuals and writers on the one hand and Orthodox clergy on the other at the Religious-Philosophical Society. Russian intellectuals and Russian clergy had been almost totally estranged since the early nineteenth century. The new rapprochement led to a religious revival in Russian culture. A part of the general cultural renascence of the period, this revival helped assert the reputations of such religious philosophers as Nikolai Berdyaev and Lev Shestov, supplied the essential religious strain in twentieth-century Russian poetry, extending from the early Blok to the late Pasternak, and had a long-range influence that can still be felt in such major works of Soviet literature as Bulgakov's *The Master and Margarita*, Pasternak's *Doctor Zhivago*, and Solzhenitsyn's *August 1914*.

Sergei Diaghilev was crushed by the defection of his lover. The center of his interest eventually shifted from painting and literature, with which he had been principally involved during his association with Filosofov, to music and ballet. In order to be away from St. Petersburg and to avoid seeing Gippius and Filosofov together, Diaghilev organized the Russian Seasons in Paris. The impact of these concerts and ballet performances on the future of music, dance, and the visual arts, both in Russia and throughout the world, is too well known to require documentation. Yet, that entire momentous miracle might never have happened if there had not been a school friendship between the young Dima Filosofov and his classmates Benois, Somov, and Nouvel.

6

The objections of Zinaida Gippius to the Tsarist autocracy was that it perpetuated the artificial division of people into social classes and, by supporting an official church and by persecuting religious dissenters and minorities, prevented each individual from seeking his or her own path to God. She saw the aim of the Russian revolutionary movement, with which she identified after the revolution of 1905 and which she came to revere, in the establishment of total universal freedom and equality in all aspects of social life. She also believed that the coming revolution would give people a freedom of choice in their pursuit of religious experience and permit alternate life-styles for those individuals for whom the traditional heterosexual family life was not suited. (Nina Berberova's book *The Italics Are Mine* draws interesting parallels between the aversion of Gippius to traditional forms of love and family life and the similar attitudes of her coeval Gertrude Stein.)

The Bolshevik victory after the October Revolution spelled the collapse of all of her hopes and aspirations. Lenin's version of the Revolution, with its insistence on the primacy of class warfare, abolition of all personal freedom, gradual restriction of interpersonal relationships to their most bourgeois forms, and, above all, its total ban on all spiritual life and religious growth, was for Gippius not merely oppression but a betrayal of all revolutionary ideals, sacrilege, and deicide. Another blow, almost as shattering as the October Revolution, was the defection of Filosofov, who after accompanying Gippius, Merezhkovsky, and Zlobin in a perilous escape to Poland that involved an illegal border-crossing in 1920, left them to join a group of revolutionaries opposed to Lenin, based in Warsaw and led by Boris Savinkov.

A member of the terrorist branch of the Socialist Revolutionary party before the Revolution, Savinkov was responsible for several spectacular political assassinations. He also had literary ambitions, in which Gippius encouraged him, going to the extent of ghostwriting his best-known novel, *The Pale Horse*. After settling in Warsaw, Filosofov became Savinkov's aide in the Polish-supported organization dedicated to the overthrow of the Bolshevik regime. Filosofov went on living in Poland even after Savinkov, who was caught by Soviet border guards, died under mysterious circumstances in a Soviet prison and his counter-revolutionary organization was disbanded. There was no way of bringing Filosofov back to the Gippius-Merezhkovsky fold, as Gippius kept hoping almost until the end of his life.

7

The highest ideal for Gippius was also the ideal of both her teacher Dostoevsky and of his antipode, Chekhov (whom Gippius, incidentally, strongly disliked): the right of every human being to inner freedom. Her relentless attacks on the Soviet regime, after she emigrated and settled in Paris, were prompted by her realization that much of the Western world was gradually coming to accept the terror and the regimentation to which the Soviet Russians were being subjected as a bona fide equivalent of liberation. Her anti-Bolshevik jeremiads and poems caused a few attacks on her in Soviet publications, most notably by Leon Trotsky (who declared in his *Literature and Revolution* that although he did not believe in witchcraft, he was convinced that Gippius was a witch) and Mayakovsky. From about 1925 on, Gippius pretty much disappeared from Soviet literary studies and the position of Soviet literary historians was that she had never existed. Her name became mentionable again in Soviet encyclopedias and reference books in the 1960s, but she is mentioned only to be denounced as a decadent and a benighted reactionary who dared disagree with Lenin and Gorky.

While a governmental policy prevents Soviet scholars from according Gippius the attention she so obviously merits, the affinity of some of her views and interests with cultural trends in the West during the 1960s has led to the rediscovery of her work by some Western scholars. Her cause has been taken up in particular by the Fink Verlag (a publishing house in Munich), which in 1972 brought out a two-volume collection of her complete poetry edited by Temira Pachmuss and which has been steadily making available in photo offset editions the other writings of Gippius, not reprinted anywhere since pre-revolutionary times. Also in 1972 the Fink Verlag brought out an excellent study of Gippius in English, *Paradox in the Religious Poetry of Zinaida Gippius* by Olga Matich, originally a doctoral thesis written at the University of California, Los Angeles, which, under appropriately suggestive chapter headings ("God," "Love," "Despair," "Devil," and "Death"), offers a balanced and objective examination of the unique, personal cosmogony and the powerful religious vision embodied in her poetry.

In addition to editing the Fink Verlag reprints, Temira Pachmuss was responsible for the recent appearance of previously unpublished writings of Gippius such as her diaries and her correspondence, both in separate books and in excerpts and selections in various Russian émigré journals in Paris and New York. Professor Pachmuss's own detailed study, *Zinaida Hippius: An Intellectual Profile* (Carbondale, Ill.: Southern Illinois University Press, 1971), while informative and containing important documentation, suffers, as do her numerous introductory essays to recent publications on Gippius, from this scholar's unwillingness to see the religiously heretical, politically radical, and sexually unconventional aspects of her subject. The constant desire of Professor Pachmuss to render Zinaida Gippius as conventional and innocuous as possible has led her not only to play down the very things that make Gippius the unique writer she is, but also to delete and censor in her editions of the diaries in English (*Between Paris and St. Petersburg*) and of the letters in Russian (*Intellect and Ideas in Action: Selected Correspondence of Zinaida Hippius*)[2] the passages that apparently shock her notions of propriety.

A careful reading of the entire *oeuvre* of Zinaida Gippius that has now been made available in Russian in the West will confirm that her contemporaries at the turn of the century were right to place her in the front rank of Russian poets of that or any time. Her ability as a playwright is also beyond dispute. Her dramatic fantasy *Sacred Blood* and the more realistic *Poppy Blossoms* (written jointly with Merezhkovsky and Filosofov, but very much

2. Munich: Wilhelm Fink Verlag, 1972.

of a piece with her other works in conception and style) hold up remarkably well. Her play *The Green Ring*, which in a brilliant production by Vsevolod Meyerhold was the major event of the 1916 theatrical season, remains to this day one of the finest genuinely revolutionary and genuinely poetic plays in the Russian language.

In her prose writings, Gippius was at her weakest in the area where Merezhkovsky was at his best and most enduring: in literary criticism. The very qualities that made her such an original thinker and poet also made her blind as a critic. Her single critical feat—her early recognition of the genius of Osip Mandelstam—was never recorded in her essays and is known to us only through the accounts of others and a brief mention in her memoirs. By and large, as a critic she expected her own kind of metaphysical subtlety from all other writers and was incapable of taking an interest in any writing that did not derive from Dostoevsky. This *parti pris* led her to condemn as frivolous and insignificant prose writers of the caliber of Anton Chekhov (who was for Gippius a provincial dullard able to describe only the animal side of human existence and devoid of any understanding of women) and Vladimir Nabokov ("a writer who has absolutely nothing to say"), and to treat with contempt almost all the important Russian post-Symbolist poets, including Mayakovsky, Sergei Esenin, Pasternak, Akhmatova, and Tsvetaeva. In the case of Tsvetaeva, the attitude of Gippius (as revealed in her recently published letters to Nina Berberova and Vladislav Khodasevich) could on occasion take the form of irrational hatred that verged on the paranoid.

Nor was Gippius able to compete with Merezhkovsky

in the field of the novel. Her two big political novels, *The Devil's Puppet* and *Tsarevich Roman*, for all the knowledgeable and sympathetic glimpses they offer of life among turn-of-the-century revolutionaries, remain pallid and ineffectual imitations of Dostoevsky's *The Possessed*. But in the prose genres where Merezhkovsky did not leave his mark, the short story and the memoir, Gippius comes into her own and produces work that is superior to anything by Merezhkovsky and as good as anything written by the Symbolist prose writers of her generation. Her book of literary memoirs *Zhivye litsa* (reprinted by Professor Pachmuss as *Living Portraits*, although either *Living Persons* or *Lifelike Faces* would have been closer to the multi-levelled meaning of the Russian title) and her biography of Merezhkovsky (published in 1951 as *Dmitry Merezhkovsky*; her original title for this book was *He and We*) are basic documents for the study of the momentous literary epoch during which Gippius lived and to which she so prominently contributed. Together with her poetry, her plays, and her diaries, these two books add up to one of the more valuable literary treasure troves of our century.

As has often been the case in the history of poetry, a personal tragedy underlies the creation of some of Zinaida Gippius's most important poetic utterances. Vladimir Zlobin's candid book, based on inside knowledge and personal observation, tells us the one-of-a-kind story of heartbreak suffered by a one-of-a-kind woman who changed the course of poetry and altered the literary sensibility in her country and who does not deserve to be forgotten.

Simon Karlinsky

A Difficult Soul:
Zinaida Gippius

by Vladimir Zlobin

Editorial Note

This book is an English translation of Vladimir Zlobin's *Tyazhelaya dusha*, published in 1970 by Victor Kamkin, Inc., Rockville, Maryland. I am grateful to the original publishers for their kind authorization of the present publication.

All interpolations in brackets are Zlobin's except the ones identified as mine by the initials S. K. Asterisked footnotes are Zlobin's, numbered footnotes mine. Both Zinaida Gippius and Vladimir Zlobin were much given to ending sentences with three periods, which in Russian indicates not an ellipsis but either a pause in the discourse or a self-interruption. These periods have been retained in English only in instances of self-interruption. They do not signify an omission.

All the poetry quoted in Zlobin's book is by Zinaida Gippius, except when identified by the author or the editor as being by other poets (e.g., by Lermontov, Pushkin, Vigny, and Ibsen). I have tried to preserve the metrical scheme of the Russian originals whenever it was possible, but have often dispensed with the rhymes. The poems in which the rhymes were systematically reproduced are the epigrams and poems in humorous doggerel, where the musical effect is more important than the precise meaning.

S. K.

things" in her book (a book which is to be published i the near future).[1] And this is not the only book about Gippius. Alla Kuhlman's doctoral dissertation is on the same subject and I know of two works on her versification—by Oleg Maslenikov[2] and James Bailey[3]. The latter is on the rhythmic structure of her verse. There are one or two other books about Gippius's poetry whose titles I do not remember. In general, Gippius has begun to arouse interest, especially in America, and much more so than Merezhkovsky[4]. And that is not accidental.

The reader, however, should not think that I do not value Gippius's literary talent. But I approach her work, especially her verse, as a kind of diary (her fourth book of verse, by the way, which was published in Berlin, is called just that: A Diary). But the subject of my book is different—not the verse of Gippius, but Gippius herself, her "difficult soul," as she called it, with which she was in continual struggle:

> At times, like children, people will find cause for cheer
> And live in happy leisure, one and all;
> O, let them laugh—it is no joy to peer
> Into the murk of my own difficult, dark soul.

1. Temira Pachmuss, Zinaida Hippius: An Intellectual Profile (Carbondale, Ill.: Southern Illinois University Press, 1971).

2. Oleg A. Maslenikov, "Spectre of Nothingness: The Privative Element in the Poetry of Zinaida Hippius," Slavic and East European Journal 19 (1960): 299–311; idem, "Description of Canonical Verse Norms in the Poetry of Zinaida Hippius," in Studies in Slavic Linguistics and Poetics in Honor of Boris O. Unbegaun, ed. Robert Magidoff et al. (New York: New York University Press, 1968), pp. 89–96.

3. James Bailey, The Versification of Zinaida Gippius (Ph.D. diss., Harvard, 1965).

4. Since the publication of Zlobin's book there have appeared two

At times, like children, people will find cause for cheer
And live in happy leisure, one and all;
O, let them laugh—it is no joy to peer
Into the murk of my own difficult, dark soul.

Z. GIPPIUS

The Author's Foreword

This book is not a biography of Zinaida Gippius in the sense biography is usually understood. In her
book *Dmitry Merezhkovsky,* originally *He and We* (this
title was changed at the request of the publisher), Gippius relates the most important events of her life. As a
general rule, all memoirs are, whatever anyone might
say, *Dichtung und Wahrheit*—fiction and truth. Some of
it is true, some of it forgotten, and some made up. Fiction, however, should not be understood as distortion
and falsification of reality. It is, rather, an artistic truth
which in some cases is closer to reality than a purely
photographic reproduction of facts. An example of this
is Leo Tolstoy's *Childhood* and *Boyhood.* Compare these
books with his exact autobiography and you will see
where the real, living Tolstoy is.

In the memoirs of Gippius it could hardly be said that
fiction prevails. But that they are works of literary art is
beyond doubt. It would scarcely be possible to add anything to them. But there are some things which Gippius
calls the "main things," which she doesn't exactly forget,
but which, rather, she consciously fails to mention. To
the uninitiated the omissions are not noticeable. But
Professor Temira Pachmuss of the University of Illinois,
to whom I opened my archives, mentions these "main

We have grown used to the icy tone, to the harsh calmness of her verse. But among twentieth-century poets there can hardly be found one equal to her in power and depth of experience. The intense passion of certain of her poems is astonishing. Where does this fire, this inhuman love and hate come from?

She fought for fullness of existence, for the right to be happy and free:

> I seek the dangerous and willful
> Convergence of all roads,
> And all that is alive and beautiful
> Does quickly come to me.
>
> And if the truth of this world's tenderness
> Is not in pity, but in love—
> Then don't presume to contradict my
> All-shattering, rebellious self.

For this "dangerous and willful convergence of all roads" the late Ariadna Tyrkova[5], author of a remarkable book on Pushkin, lashed out at me. I was careless enough to publish in one of my articles an intimate note to Gippius from Filosofov. This outraged Tyrkova. My fellow writer, the poet and critic Yury Terapiano[6], also disapproved. His article "Gippius in Memoriam," in *Russian*

---

substantial new studies of Merezhkovsky by American scholars, *D. S. Merezhkovsky and the Silver Age* by Bernice Rosenthal and *The Seeker: D. S. Merezhkovsky* by C. Harold Bedford, both published in 1975.

5. Ariadna Tyrkova-Williams, a onetime prominent revolutionary activist and, later, a civic leader and journalist during her emigration.

6. The émigré poet and critic Yury Terapiano, whose book of memoirs *Vstrechi* [*Encounters*] (New York: Chekhov Publishing House, 1953) contains several sections on Gippius, Merezhkovsky, and their Paris circle.

Thought,[7] no. 2386, Nov. 13, 1965, is obviously aimed
at me. Terapiano wrote: "Since her death, much has been
written about Gippius's attitude toward love, sometimes
disgracefully immodestly, even to the point of publishing the most intimate of her letters and letters to her."
What was I to do? I do not have the right to burn these
letters. I turned for advice to another of my colleagues,
George Ivask, a professor of the University of Washington.[8] He resolutely answered: "Publish them in fifty
years." That's easy to say, in fifty years. But what will
it be like in fifty years? Professor Wladimir Weidlé[9] once
jokingly said in a conversation that in the year 2000
mankind will celebrate the third millennium of Christianity with the issuance of a stamp depicting Christ
with the inscription "Visit Jerusalem."

I have great respect for Professor Weidlé, but he is a
romantic and an optimist. No, I would paint a different
picture: not only will there be no stamps of Christ, but
even if on that day He Himself descended from heaven to
earth, he wouldn't be noticed. He wouldn't be put into
prison and the Grand Inquisitor would not come to con-
verse with Him. At best He would end up in a Salvation
Army palace where, after being disinfected, He would be
fed as if in the best restaurant and put to bed in a marble
bunk.

"Will the Son of Man, having come, find faith on

7. *Russkaja Mysl'*, a Russian-language newspaper, published in
Paris.
8. George (Yury) Ivask, a noted émigré poet and literary scholar,
in recent years Professor of Russian Literature at Amherst.
9. Wladimir Weidlé has published a number of books on art and
literary history both in French and in Russian.

earth?"[10] And not fifty years, but only thirty-three years separate us from that.

Oh, certainly an extraordinary future awaits mankind. One cannot even conceive of the things people will invent. But of the humanities, of art, of music and poetry nothing will remain. The onset of the new ice age can already be felt. More and more often the so-called beatniks, the first victims, can be glimpsed in the crowd— lost boys with long hair and crazed eyes.

And so I made a decision: in spite of the criticism, which is in essence well meaning, my book about Gippius will appear without a single omission. Not one word will be crossed out or replaced by another.

Let the book be full of contradictions, of the most impossible, the most improbable surprises. That does not bother me. Thus it will all the more clearly reflect the living soul of Gippius, her bond with life and her will to struggle.

Zinaida Gippius has the right to freedom of speech and woe unto him who infringes on that right.

1965

10. Luke 18:8

ONE

Gippius and Merezhkovsky

The twenty years that have passed since the death of Zinaida Nikolaevna Gippius (she died in Paris on September 9, 1945) are not such a long time, but they seem like an eternity. By now, we remember almost nothing about her. And how could we remember? What do we know about her? A few superficial, not always important facts which she related in her book on Merezhkovsky. But even there she tried to talk about herself as little as possible, deliberately relegating herself to the background. She did that, incidentally, not from modesty—she knew her own worth—but from a desire, which she herself did not quite understand, to remain in the shadows. One cannot but regret this: as an individual, as a poet and a writer she is a phenomenon no less significant, no less original than Merezhkovsky, who had eclipsed her with his celebrity.

The fate of this woman was unusual. Indeed, between the Zinaida Gippius we know and the one she really was there is a chasm. She left behind notebooks, diaries, letters. But most important, she left us her poems. They are her real autobiography. In them is her whole life without embellishment, with all its frustrations and soaring hopes. But you must know how to read them. If you do not have the key, it is better not to touch them, because you will end up in a labyrinth from which there is no exit.

She was born on November 8, 1869, in the town of Belev, of a consumptive father, whose family emigrated from Germany to Moscow in the sixteenth century, and a marvelous Siberian woman, Anastasia Stepanova.

> Maidenly March did not shine at my dawn,
> Its fires were lit in stern November.

A strange little girl, unlike the others. So tiny in a pink knitted sweater with the last button always unbuttoned. And so serious looking.

She adored her parents. Her attachment to them was so passionate that when at her father's insistence she was sent to a boarding school in Kiev she couldn't endure the separation, fell ill, and spent almost all her time in the school infirmary. Separation was for her worse than death:

> You who are living, beware separations,

she would write later, knowing from childhood that

> Love will not bear it without revenge,
> Love will withdraw its gifts.

"Since my childhood I have been wounded by death and love," she noted in 1922 in "A Concluding Word." In her book on Merezhkovsky she wrote about her father: "I loved him so much that sometimes, looking at his tall figure in a short fox fur coat, with his back leaning against the stove, I would think, 'What if he should suddenly die? Then I will die too.'"

He died when she had scarcely turned eleven. But even earlier, in connection with the death in their home of a distant woman relative, she wrote, "Death then took possession of my soul for the rest of my life." It was as if the death of her father was the beginning of her own death which she experienced then for the first time in all its knowable reality. She was hardly born when she had already begun to die. Small wonder that her nickname at school in Kiev was "the little person with the large grief."

Next to her parents she loved most of all her one and only Nanny Dasha—Darya Pavlovna Sokolova:

She will never know	I loved her gray dress,
How I loved her,	Every lock of her hair.
How that love pierced	But even if I could tell her,
My whole existence.	She wouldn't understand.

Nanny Dasha called her "my little white priest" and would carry her in her arms around the hall before putting her to bed. It was she who took her for walks in the Summer Gardens. Gippius's father twice tried to settle in the capital, but he couldn't take the Petersburg climate and had himself transferred to the provinces, the second time to Nezhin, Gogol's town, where he soon afterward died of acute tuberculosis.

"The first time we lived there was when I was only four years old," was the way Gippius recalled her "first St. Petersburg." "I remember only the carriages we rode in and the statue of Krylov in the Summer Gardens where Nanny Dasha took me and where lots of children played. And there was also Sestroretsk, the forest, the sea, and the tiny white snowflakes that fell on my white coat (in May)."

I was dressed much too warmly,
My braid under a hood.
I go out—it's not summer now—
For half an hour at most.

But once, Nanny Dasha took her not to the Summer Gardens, but to the Gostinny Dvor shopping arcade to buy her a doll. It was the end of March. Not tiny snowflakes fell on her coat, but large flakes of wet snow that looked like dirty handkerchiefs. Disappointment awaited the "little person," the first of her life, that "knock against the wall, the wall through which we will pass perhaps only after death," as she later put it. Instead of a doll she set her heart on a real live little girl she saw at the store. So much so that Nanny Dasha could get her home only with difficulty. "My desires were more precious to me than anything else."

In this first desire of hers is focused everything which she dreamed of later in life and which she could not, did not know how to forego (or perhaps simply did not want to forego in the depths of her soul). Several weeks before her death, on the jacket of a book she was leafing through—the anthology of Russian émigré verse, *The Anchor*—she, half-paralyzed, scratched out with her left hand, from right to left so that it could be read only in a mirror:

> On the staircase . . . The steps, ever more ethereal,
> Run up or down—isn't it all the same?
> And with each step my heart grows colder
> And everything that was—was long ago.

This last helpless attempt to overcome her own weakness is one of the innumerable proofs of her extraordinary tenacity of life.

The fire of our souls is inextinguishable.

But who could have guessed that in the fragile, ephemeral, otherworldly being she seemed to be, there was such strength?

II

Her first confession . . . She described it in
"A Concluding Word." A poor, rustic-looking church.
Green treetops, seen through the high windows. Silence.
Springtime. (And how is it that up to now no critic has
noted her remarkable language—clear, witty, sparkling
like a diamond of the purest water?) She wrote about this
first confession: "But I still don't understand redemp-
tion." And she added, "Obviously, I don't understand
repentance either."

Now, when her "works and days" are well known,
that confession is especially surprising, not to say stag-
gering. There is not one piece of evidence, not even a
hint of evidence, that even once in her long life she sincerely repented of anything, yielded, admitted she was at
fault, or even simply asked forgiveness from anyone or
apologized. There was neither humility nor repentance.
It was as if she feared that, having humbled herself and
repented, she would lose that inner support, that
mainspring hidden from her consciousness, which en-
abled her, for better or worse, to stay on the surface while
others sank to the bottom like a stone.

> But I will not give up my soul
> To the weakness of humility . . .
> I will not give Thee humility,
> It is the lot of slaves.

In her book on Merezhkovsky she recalled that when
her father was displeased with her, he would cease to pay
her any attention and she knew it was unavoidable (her
word) that she ask for his forgiveness. But she says nothing of the effort that it cost her. The fact that she would
go and ask forgiveness testifies to her truly limitless love
for her father.

She began to write poetry at the age of seven. Here is her first poem:

> For a long time I have not known sadness.
> For a long time I have shed no tears.
> I have helped no one,
> Nor have I loved anyone.
>
> Love people and you'll come to grief.
> It is impossible to help everyone.
> The world is like the deep blue sea
> And I forgot it long ago.

For comparison, here is another, written at the end of her life:

> I have narrowed it all to one thought,
> While I peer into the shimmering murk
> And for a long time I've needed no one,
> Just as no one has needed me.

The same theme, the same meter, with the invariable masculine gender, and the same attitude toward the world—offended and contemptuous, like Lermontov's Demon.[1]

In her book on Merezhkovsky she defines her nature thus: "Once something is given, it doesn't matter what, it remains with me, always the same. The bud may blos-

---

1. The hero of Mikhail Lermontov's long narrative poem "The Demon," which is set in the Caucasus and describes the love of a Byronic devil for the Georgian princess Tamara, whom he kills with his kiss once she is able to respond to his love. The conception of Lermontov's poem owed a great deal to "Éloa ou la soeur des anges" by Alfred de Vigny, which Zlobin mentions later on. The numerous quotations from Lermontov later on in this chapter are all from "The Demon." The masculine gender mentioned by Zlobin is expressed in Russian in past tense verbs which have to agree in gender with the subject of the sentence, in this case the pronoun *I*.

som forth, but it is the same flower, nothing new can be added to it."

Everything she knew and felt at seventy she had known and felt at seven, when she hadn't been able to express it. "Every love is defeated, is swallowed by death," she wrote at the age of fifty-three in "A Concluding Word." And if as a child of four she cried so bitterly over her first disappointment in love ("the living doll"), it was because she came to feel with the utmost acuteness that *there will be no love,* just as she felt after the death of her father that she too would die.

No less interesting is her second poem written two years later, when she was nine:

> Enough of this languishing longing,
> Enough of this hopeless wait!
> It's time to make peace with heaven,
> And begin my life after death.

Lermontov has:

> I want to make my peace with heaven.

Even if she had read "The Demon" at the age of nine, which is not impossible, this is not an imitation. In 1905 [1893—S. K.] she wrote:

> I'm close to God, and yet I cannot pray,
> And I want love, but cannot love a soul.

Lermontov has:

> I want to make my peace with heaven,
> I want to love, I want to pray.

And there are many such coincidences. No wonder she was so drawn to Lermontov. She knew several of his poems by heart, while at the same time, with a very few exceptions, she never remembered her own.

About her childhood and early youth we know almost nothing. The times in which she was born and grew up, the 1870s and 1880s, left no imprint on her. From the very beginning of her days she lived as if outside time and space, concerned almost from the cradle with solving the "eternal questions." She herself ridiculed this in one of her parodies, a genre in which she was a master:

> I tried to solve—the problem is immense—
> I followed logic to its very brink,
> I tried to solve: In what especial sense
> Are noumenon and phenomenon linked?

Social issues? What a bore! So, when the twenty-three-year-old Merezhkovsky appeared on her horizon with his abstract humanism and his, even for that time, mediocre verse, she instinctively recoiled from him. After all, not only were his verses mediocre, he didn't know how to ride and he didn't dance.

She was a person of passions, and passions awoke in her early. She would learn how to control herself to perfection, but she didn't learn that all at once. Even as a child she could lie, pretending to be dangerously ill. Her mother, whom she loved more than anything in the world, suffered because of this. But she tormented her and she tormented herself. For what was she yearning?

> I need what is not in this world.

That line made the rounds through the whole of literary Russia and with it began the fame of Gippius as a poet. But what was she, a living person, to do with that unpalatable, stone-hard ideal? Really, what could she be yearning for? She did not confess. She only mentioned in passing that

> Strange dreams at times descend on me.

How were they strange? Why? She was silent. But Lermontov answered for her:

> I will fly down to you
> . . . .
> And on your silken lashes
> I will waft golden dreams.

In the poem "Griselda," written at about the same time as "I need what is not in this world," she said that someone did appear to her either in a dream or in waking, for she asks with surprise:

> O, tell me, wisest Tempter,
> Dark Spirit, could you be
> The misconstrued Preceptor
> Who teaches us Beauty?

Is there behind all this some sort of reality? I will talk about that later. But in those years, in the days of her early youth, the problem of evil did not disturb her too much. When she met Merezhkovsky she still didn't know, hadn't yet decided whether she was the Madonna or a witch. Both possibilities attracted her. She did not, however, hurry with the decision because both principles coexisted splendidly within her. And what Merezhkovsky liked more than anything else was the combination of opposites.

III

Their encounter was a unique event in her life. She considered it providential and she was right. They were indeed created for each other. But not in the way this is usually understood, that is, not in the romantic sense. To compare them to Philemon and Baucis, to

Daphnis and Chloe, or to Afanasy Ivanovich and Pulcheria Ivanovna[2] is to show either naiveté or ignorance.

They met in Borzhom[3] one Sunday at the end of June, 1888, at a dance in the rotunda. One of her schoolboy admirers introduced Merezhkovsky to her. "I greeted him rather drily," she wrote in her memoirs, "and from the very first we started to—well, not exactly quarrel, but something like it." Before they met she had come upon a copy of *The Pictorial Review* with some of his poems, which she didn't like. And he, after coming to Borzhom, happened to see her portrait, at the sight of which he exclaimed: "What a mug!"

"However, after the first encounter we began to see each other daily," she continued. "But almost every conversation turned into an argument."

With the schoolboys she was much freer, happier, and, most important, calmer. There wasn't the constant tension and fear which she for some reason experienced in the presence of Merezhkovsky and which troubled her. "It is curious that I had a moment of fear," she admitted. "I wanted those encounters to end, wanted him to leave the town. What was I to do with him?"

She had already been in love, and more than once. She knew what it was, but here was something completely different. She came right out and said it: "And here, with Merezhkovsky, for the first time in my life something unlike anything else happened to me."

The "something unlike anything else" took place as if by itself, without the participation of her will. On the eleventh of July, on a moonlit night during a dance at

2. The chaste and patriarchal married couple in Gogol's story "Old-World Landowners."

3. Borzhom is a popular mineral-water spa in the southern Caucasus.

the rotunda, she and Merezhkovsky somehow came to be alone in the park on the path which winds along the banks of the Borzhomka River. "I cannot remember how our strange conversation began," she wrote in describing that nocturnal stroll. "The strangest part of all was that he no longer seemed strange to me. I had more than once been offered a proposal, as they say, and even more often had heard declarations of love. But this was not a proposal or a declaration. We—and it is important that it was both of us—suddenly began to speak as if it had been decided long ago that we would marry and that it would be good if we did."

In the same way, without the participation of her will, as if in a dream, the wedding ceremony took place "by itself" in Tiflis on the morning of January 8, 1889. "I was either calm or in a stupor," she said. "It seemed to me that none of it was very serious."

That evening Merezhkovsky left for his hotel and she went to bed forgetting that she was married. The next morning she could hardly remember it, when her mother called through the door, "You're still sleeping and your husband is already here. Get up!"

And she exclaimed in a Flaubertian tone: "My husband? How astonishing!"

IV

What would have become of them if they hadn't met? He probably would have married a merchant's daughter, sired numerous children and written historical novels in the manner of Danilevsky.[4] She . . .

4. Grigory Danilevsky (1829–1890), author of popular historical romances, set for the most part in the eighteenth century.

but it's harder to tell with her. Because of her courage and dynamism she had more options. A sportswoman, she loved risk and strove to do everything to the limit. That is, precisely what he was totally incapable of. As it stated in his passport: "Judged unfit for military service."

Perhaps she would have rested immobile for a long time, sinking into the sand, an unexploded bomb. And then she suddenly would have exploded to no purpose from an accidental jolt, killing several innocent bystanders. Or perhaps she wouldn't have exploded: a technical specialist, someone on the order of Riurik Eduardovich Occasioner,* would have saved her by spiritually defusing her, and she would have continued to spend her time in the delightful company of schoolboys and young poets. One can fantasize on this theme endlessly. But one thing is certain: her marriage to Merezhkovsky, whatever one thinks of that marriage, was their salvation. It saved them both from falling into insignificance, from metaphysical nonexistence.

Several weeks after the wedding they left for St. Petersburg, where they settled in a small apartment on Vereyskaya Street and later in the famous Muruzi House on the corner of Liteyny Prospect and Panteleymonovskaya Street. Their life together lasted for almost fifty-three years, until his death.

Strange as it may seem, at least at first glance, the guiding male role belonged not to him, but to her. She was very feminine and he masculine, but on the creative and metaphysical plane their roles were reversed. She fer-

*The name for the Devil in one of her unpublished stories called "Probably."

tilized, while he gestated and gave birth. She was the seed, and he the soil, the most fertile of all black earths. In that sense and that sense alone, he was an exceptional, unprecedented, unique phenomenon. His productivity was astonishing. Gippius discerned his true nature, the feminine principle concealed within him, and only through inexperience—she was after all only nineteen years old—did she not sense the inner weakness beneath the external brilliance that dazzled "literary" Borzhom (which in any case was not difficult to dazzle). His receptivity, his ability to assimilate ideas verged on the miraculous. He "listened with the pores of his skin," as she put it, and in comparison to him she lacked subtlety. But she had ideas, or rather had a certain, still unclear, still unexpressed reality, resembling nothing else, not even Paradise. A new planet. "What clear, vivid dreams" was all she could say.

He listened carefully to her poetry and justly valued his morning walks with her in the Borzhom park. She also loved them. In those walks, conversations, and even in their quarrels was the beginning of their convergence, of their spiritual marriage whose progeny would be as numerous as the sands of the sea.

In the first year after their marriage, in Petersburg, there occurred one important change: he gave up poetry and started to write prose. She did not give up poetry (she never would), but she also devoted more of her time to prose. This was not her first attempt. Earlier she had written diaries, not to mention letters (which were often exemplars of epistolary art). Now she wrote prose mostly for money in order to give Merezhkovsky a chance to work freely on his first novel, *Julian the Apostate*.

Where did it come from, this *Julian* and its sequel

Leonardo da Vinci, the second novel in the now famous trilogy? "The idea of 'duality' which he developed in *Leonardo* seemed to me to be false," she wrote in her memoirs. "And I strove to prove that to him." Which is strange, for the idea was hers and he took it from her:

> O, tell me, wisest Tempter,
> Dark Spirit, could you be
> The misconstrued Preceptor
> Who teaches us Beauty?

Both *Julian* and *Leonardo* emerged from those four lines, the kernel she accidently let fall. But while Merezhkovsky was still entranced with "duality" ("the abyss above and the abyss below"), she had already moved away from that idea, absorbed by another one which later became the most important idea of his life.

That she tried to explain these time lags of his (which are understandable: even in the spiritual plane one does not give birth without gestation) proves that she did not understand their relationship. It seemed to her that the same ideas were in him inherently, but that it took him longer to become conscious of them. He had experienced, according to her theory, a "slow and constant *growth* [the italics are hers] in one and the same direction, but there was, as it were, a succession of phases, a change (without betrayal of the idea)." A succession of phases? But it was not a matter of gestation, it was a matter of fertilization. Had she been so firmly convinced of the independent genesis of his ideas, she would not have constantly searched for proof of it.

Of course, one cannot say that she was responsible for each one of his lines. She gave him the most important thing—the idea. Then it was up to him. He was free to formulate and develop it in his own way. His role was no less significant than hers, no less responsible. Only it is not the role that is usually ascribed to him. If it is difficult to establish the precise moment of physical conception, then the moment of spiritual conception is utterly elusive.

V

"As for me, that summer [1905] I suddenly became absorbed in one idea which became for me a sort of *idée fixe*, and my *idée fixe* was the 'trinitarian structure of the world.'" This was the very idea which ripened in her while Merezhkovsky was still absorbed in "duality."

He seized upon the new idea at once. Of course! He understood it "so totally, so viscerally," Gippius rejoiced, "that clearly the idea was already in him but had not yet reached the level of his awareness." How modest she was! This idea almost cost her the salvation of her soul and if she didn't perish, it was only by a miracle. But it made no difference to her. She had accomplished the deed of her lifetime. It was now his turn. And, as her notes testify, he rose to the occasion.

"He gave to it [to that idea] all its fullness, he transformed it in the very depths of his heart and mind, turning it into the religious idea of his life and faith—*The Idea of the Trinity, the Coming of the Holy Ghost, and of the Third Kingdom or Testament* [the italics are hers]. All the writings of his last decades contain this and only this principal, underlying foundation, this central idea."

One could not put it more clearly. Of course it does not make a single one of the sixty-two volumes of Merezhkovsky's collected works a book by Gippius. But that changes nothing. Their recipe is no one's concern. It is a personal, intimate matter. And thank God Merezhkovsky the writer had such an intelligent wife.

There is one other proof of Gippius's influence on the work of Merezhkovsky—a certain odor completely uncharacteristic of him—

> As if a rotten egg had broken open
> Or a quarantine guard were fumigating with sulfur[5]

—which sometimes wafts from his ostensibly pious writings. When in 1903 Pobedonostsev[6] banned the meetings of the Petersburg Religious-Philosophical Society[7], one of the reasons, perhaps, was that elusive odor which he sensed in the atmosphere of freedom that prevailed at the meetings.

For the first session of this society, which took place on November 29, 1901, in the hall of the Geographical Society on the Fontanka, Gippius had a black, seemingly modest dress especially made. It was designed in such a way that, with the slightest movement, the pleats would part and a pale pink lining would show through. The impression was that she was naked underneath. She

5. Quotation from Alexander Pushkin's parody of Dante, "And on We Went, and Fear Embraced Me" (1832).

6. Konstantin Pobedonostsev, the sinister, arch-reactionary advisor to Nicholas II.

7. The impact of the St. Petersburg Religious-Philosophical Society sessions in 1901–1902 on subsequent developments in Russian culture has been eloquently described by Sergei Makovsky in the opening chapter of his *On the Parnassus of the Silver Age* and by Gippius herself in the chapter on Vasily Rozanov in her memoir *Living Portraits*. A German book was recently devoted to this topic: Jutta Scherrer, *Die Petersburger Religiös-Philosophischen Vereinigungen*, Forschungen zur Osteuropeischen Geschichte, vol. 19 (Wiesbaden: Osteuropa Institut, Freie Universität Berlin, 1973).

would often recall that dress with evident pleasure, even at an age when, it would seem, it was time to forget such things. Either because of that dress or because of some of her other whimsies, the displeased church dignitaries who took part in the meetings nicknamed her the "white she-devil." But that was a mere display of bad taste and of flippancy. Her close relationship with the Devil expressed itself differently.

Did she believe in God? The question seems out of place. But upon closer acquaintance with her "works and days," it arises of its own accord. But it cannot be given a simple answer. What can be said with certainty is that she believed in the Devil. That is certain. She believed in him exactly the way Gogol and Dostoevsky did, and the way Tolstoy *did not*. The Devil was for her a real being, one of the most important, if not the most important in her cast of characters. In her writings, however, he remains for the most part in the shadows, behind the scenes, and shows himself only rarely, in those instances when the story or poem is devoted to him.* But it is impossible to imagine a serious metaphysical letter or conversation of hers where the theme of the Devil does not occupy a central position.

She herself related how, in her youth, she once had a necklace made out of the wedding rings of her married admirers. An echo of this is found in her poem "Wisdom," where she, in the guise of a she-devil, "stole love from two lovers":

> They sit there, kissing. But I run
> Right up to them and quickly snatch it!
> Now it is probably no fun
> For them to hold and kiss each other.

*For example, in the story "Ivan Ivanovich and the Devil."

This is what the "misconstrued Preceptor" had taught her. With the same flippancy with which she would describe the cabaret singer's dress that she devised for the Religious-Philosophical Society, she cited in her memoirs a remark she made after her wedding ceremony: "It seems to me that nothing special has happened." To which one of the ushers replied, "Oh, no, something did happen, and it *is* serious."

Of that she was, incidentally, convinced soon enough. "No, Dima, I cannot love you the way I love Dmitry" (letter to Filosofov, 1905). "We are, after all, one being," she said of herself and Merezhkovsky even after his death. This is both incomprehensible and unpleasant, but it represented a definite reality. If one imagines Merezhkovsky as a tall tree with branches reaching to the clouds, then the roots of that tree are Gippius. And the deeper the roots grow into the ground, the higher the branches reach into the sky. Some of the branches now seem to touch Paradise. And no one so much as suspected that she was in hell.

VI

The Merezhkovskys spent the summer of 1905 at a dacha on the Kobrino estate along the Warsaw railroad line. From there she sent a thirty-two-page letter to Filosofov. He lived with them at the time but had gone for a month to his own estate to visit his mother. That letter does credit not only to her intelligence but also to the courage with which she bared her soul. "Do you know or could you clearly imagine," she asked Filosofov, "what a *cold* person is [the italics are hers], a cold spirit, a cold soul, a cold body, everything cold, the whole being at once? It isn't death, because next to it, inside the person, exists a sense of that cold—its 'burn'—I cannot say it any other way. Death is preferable if it is simply nonexistence and its cold is only the absence of all warmth. But this cold is the cold of condensed air and this existence is like the existence in Dante's inferno, remember, in that lake of ice." That was when she finally learned what that fire of snow was for which her soul had yearned with "vatic irrepressibility":

> With vatic irrepressibility
> My soul is yearning for the fire of snow.

Because of this there sometimes wafted from the Merezhkovskys such coldness—the coldness of interplanetary space—that it froze the souls of those clinging to them as sparrows freeze on telegraph wires in a hard winter frost. But the suffering that this coldness caused them was realized by no one.

"Even if you will not understand, believe me, Dima," she continued, "that it is a very great suffering. I am cold, or we are cold, we are pure cold, already without any trace, without any likeness of the constantly perceptible and perceived forward-moving love for humanity, people, or the world. We are without pity, without softness, without tenderness. That is why we suffer so. You remember those "eternal torments" of Father Zosima's hell, his words about the soul that already knows love is deliverance, that understands love, that sees it—and yet cannot love.[8] I live in that hell now on earth."

One can only marvel that she didn't lose her mind.

---

8. From Father Zosima's mystical sermon on hell and hellfire, which is a part of his vita, purportedly written by Alyosha Karamazov in Book Six of Dostoevsky's *The Brothers Karamazov*.

Even if we limit her existence in the "lake of ice" to the period from 1905 to 1922 (when she finally said, "Enough!"), even then we come up with seventeen years. And in the "lake of ice" each minute is an eternity.

But it is here that we begin to understand her extraordinary life force as well as her healthy religious instinct. It would seem that this would be the best time to think about personal salvation. Just then, just there in hell is when one is concerned with one's own skin. But no: *she did not think of herself first*. "I feel," she said, "that this has to be expressed not in words, so as to make another's soul understand." She was only one out of many. "I speak about myself, but I speak with courage, with the full right to speak, knowing both through inner insight and factually, realistically, that I am not the only soul who suffers in this manner. There are others, too, many others now, and later there will be more of them."

She instinctively knew that the cause of salvation was a general, *collective* cause. This truth was known to her. But only there, in hell, did it reveal itself to her fully and acquire a new, unexpected, uniquely valid meaning. All creatures will be saved; and if all are included, then the Devil will also be saved, for he, too, is a creature created by God. So she prayed for the Devil.

For good Christians this was blasphemy, and her hell was an abstraction. She spoke of it too much and too cerebrally. In hell one either groans or is silent. But we are poor Christians and what we really fear is heaven, not hell. Heaven, given the existence of the eternal torments or even of a single sinner, be he justly condemned, is not entirely heaven, that is, not heaven. What separates us from true heaven, from "universal harmony," is an inexpressible horror: the justification of evil.

But Gippius was fearless and here, as in everything, took things to their logical conclusion. Her disquisitions on hell may have been lengthy, but she also knew when to hold her peace if necessary. She did not state and would not state the most important thing, no matter how much one questioned her. But if there is even a drop of audacity in us, we can fill in the picture she began.

The Devil fell asleep in hell and dreamt of Paradise:

> And memories of better days
> Crowded before him in a swarm.
> Of days when in the dwelling of light
> He shone, a pure cherub.
> . . . .
>
> When he believed and loved,
> The happy first-born of creation.[9]

Nowhere did she say directly that he would be saved, perhaps because she did not know everything after all. But together with him she hoped:

> Everything was decided by the Holy Ghost,
> He holds the keys of all fates,
> He will save everyone . . .

Universal harmony? That was the heavenly music which she heard in hell over the porcine wheezing of the Devil. She wouldn't trade it for anything in the world, not for any white raiment, or any earthly or heavenly miracles.

Merezhkovsky died never guessing that his celebrated idea of the Third Kingdom of God which, according to Gippius, he made "the religious idea of all his life and faith," was actually *the Devil's dream of universal harmony*. But it was just this profound, subterranean, almost

9. From Lermontov's "The Demon."

anti-Christian substructure that was Merezhkovsky's particular strength. Compared to other builders of the "City of God," abstract idealists all, he had the advantage that the others built on sand, or started with the cupola, while he descended to a depth where the stable foundations of the "City of God" could be laid out: to the depths of hell, to the bottom of the "lake of ice."

His luxuriant, unexpected flowering right after their flight from Russia lasted around fifteen years, from 1920 to 1935. It was precisely this period that was a period of decline for Gippius. A kind of daze seems to have overcome her. She plunged into complete hopelessness, sinking to the very bottom of the "lake of ice."

In 1905 she still had hope or "a hope for hope," as she put it in that same letter sent to Filosofov at Bogdanovskoe.[10] "Torment that seems eternal to us cannot be eternal, because after the instant when we sense its eternity, the soul is granted in the next instant a hope for hope of escape."

But now she no longer had even that. Time for her seemed to freeze at the point when she realized that the torment was eternal:

> A single moment froze and lasted
> Like eternal repentance.
> Never to cry, never to pray.
> Despair. Despair.

Once she had lightheartedly declared:

> I accept my lot—victory and love.

But now there was neither victory nor liberation, only an icy prison where she sat and suffered in astonishment

---

10. The country estate of the Filosofov family.

like a plucked bird of paradise. "Suffering can be forgiven only by tearing oneself away from life," she noted in "A Concluding Word." "For all suffering comes from love, all kinds of love, conscious and unconscious as well, because all love (all life) is loss."

Did she ever really believe in love or did this lapse overtake her only later, in eternity?

> Someone from the darkness of silence
> Summoned to the cold earth,
> Summoned out of sleep and silence
> My captive soul.

In her first extant diary she noted in March, 1893, "Yes, I believe in love as a great force, as an earthly miracle. I believe, but I know that there are no miracles and there will be none." Thirty years later in "A Concluding Word" she carried that thought to its conclusion: "Every love will be conquered, will be devoured by death." Death: that was a cloud advancing upon her from the depths of eternity and concealing from her the sun of love. She greedily caught its rare, dim, momentary rays:

> Lord, My Lord, Sun, where art Thou?
> Help my captive soul.

But her prayer was not answered. She still had almost twenty years to live. But she had nothing more to do on earth:

> No words, no tears, no sighs, nothing—
> The earth and mankind don't deserve them.

And she respectfully gave back to God her ticket, her "invitation to a beheading."[11] Again Lermontov comes to mind:

11. Zlobin fuses the oft-quoted image from Dostoevsky's *The*

And the defeated Demon cursed
His mad dreams.
And he remained alone in the universe,
Haughty as before,
Without hope or love.[12]

Brothers Karamazov about "returning the ticket to the Maker" with the title of Vladimir Nabokov's novel.

12. From Lermontov's "The Demon."

TWO

Miss Tification

It is amazing the way legends that have nothing in common with reality arise around the names of well known people, to say nothing of celebrities. One needn't go far for an example: Zinaida Gippius. It is for some reason generally assumed that she was distracted, muddleheaded, always confused, and unable to cope at all with everyday matters. In short, she was an absentminded intellectual, along the lines of Professor A. A. Meyer, who for a long time couldn't figure out why his feet hurt. They hurt because he had put on two left boots.

Boris Zaitsev in his book on Chekhov[1] depicted her more or less in that manner, but with added decadent languor and the inevitable "mermaid eyes." Chekhov on his first trip abroad travelling with the celebrated Suvorin[2] encountered the Merezhkovskys in Venice. Gippius apparently told him (Zaitsev conveys their conversation as a dialogue) that they paid eighteen francs a week for room and board. At least that's what Chekhov understood and he hastened to write his sister in Moscow about it. Later it turned out that they paid eighteen francs a day, not a week. Gippius got it wrong, Zaitsev pointed

---

1. Boris Zaitsev, *Chekhov* (New York: Chekhov Publishing House, 1954). See also note 6 to Chapter 7.

2. The ultra-conservative publisher and playwright Alexei Suvorin, Chekhov's close friend and the addressee of Chekhov's most significant personal letters.

out, because "she was just as confused in her youth as she was in her old age in Paris."

Actually Gippius didn't get anything wrong, she had deceived Chekhov on purpose. "I never forget anything," she wrote in one of her last poems. She remembered figures especially well and, given the occasion, would boast of it. She liked figures:

> Do you know why I'm happy?
> I am again among my sweet numbers.
> How calm it is among figures and measures.
> Their eternal world is quiet and harmonious.

The funds on which the Merezhkovskys travelled at that time were limited. They kept track of expenses and Gippius always kept the accounts. There is no doubt she knew the rates of the *pensione* in Venice. She decided to play a joke on Chekhov, since the occasion had presented itself. She generally loved to mystify people. This trait, that few knew about, gave her something in common with Alexei Remizov,[3] of all people. It was not for nothing that it was said of her that she was an Englishwoman named Miss Tification.

Chekhov, who was delighted by everything abroad, and particularly by the low prices, amused her and, it seems, annoyed her a little. In her memoir *Living Portraits*, however, she not unkindly related how in Venice he kept wanting to stretch out on the grass.[4] It's too bad

3. Alexei Remizov, a highly original and influential prose writer who lived in Paris after the Revolution.

4. In his letter to Alexei Suvorin of March 23, 1895, Chekhov wrote: "Give my best to Italy. I love her passionately, even though you did tell Grigorovich that I lay down in the middle of St. Mark's Square and said, 'How good it would be to stretch on the grass somewhere near Moscow.'" The letter was included in Maria Chekhova's

Zaitsev didn't reread those pages of Gippius. He probably wouldn't have learned anything new about Chekhov, but he might have learned a little about Gippius, about her memory, for example.

It is easy to imagine how the mix-up came about. What is important about this joke is its meaning, which was: "So I was mistaken, but you, Anton Pavlovich, should have been able to figure out yourself that it is impossible for the two of us to live in Venice in a good hotel with full board and lodging on 60 kopecks a day, no matter how low the prices."

One of Gippius's frequent victims was Merezhkovsky. Once, during their emigration in Paris, a certain lady who at one time used to visit them on Sundays sent them as a gift a novel she had written for some unknown reason. It was called *The Intermittent Thread* and was most peculiar. Several days later, when Merezhkovsky sat down to write her a thank you note (which he rarely did), it turned out that he didn't know her name or patronymic. He asked Gippius. She looked at him with undisguised contempt: "Oh, Dmitry, you never know anything. She's called Emilia Dionysievna."

"Dionysievna?" he asked again. "You mean, she's actually called Dionysievna?"

"Why, yes. What's so strange about that?"

Of course the woman was not named Emilia, much less Dionysievna. Gippius had made it up. But Merezhkovsky, believing her completely and having no under-

---

1912–1916 edition of her brother's letters, which Gippius knew and quoted. Writing in the early 1920s about her and Merezhkovsky's encounter with Chekhov in 1891, Gippius cited the passage from Chekhov's letter to Suvorin of 1895 as if it were an actual statement Chekhov had made in 1891.

standing of jokes, went ahead and wrote: "Most respected Emilia Dionysievna."

Another time Gippius made Merezhkovsky a "present" of two of her poems which he particularly liked. Prefacing one with a long epigraph from the Apocalypse, he included them in a collection of his verse. But, forgetting about the "present," Gippius also printed the poems in her book. It is curious that no one has noticed this "joke." But that the poems are by Gippius is immediately apparent. Among Merezhkovsky's poems they are like living roses among paper flowers.

In emigration she once submitted through Georgy Adamovich[5] several poems under the name V. Vitovt to the journal *The New Ship*, to which she was a regular contributor. One of them was printed in the second issue. But it was discovered quite by accident that Gippius wrote them. She apparently didn't expect that the poems would be printed and had wanted to embarrass the overly fastidious editors by announcing that she was Vitovt.

With her friend the Swedish artist Greta Gerell, who was visiting them in Paris, Gippius would play hide-and-seek like a child, concealing herself behind the curtains.[6] A photograph from 1907 shows Gippius with several friends, making faces and sticking out her tongue. Another one of her innocent pranks took place one morning at the Villa Evelyne that the Merezhkovskys

5. Georgy Adamovich, émigré poet and literary critic, theoretician of the so-called Paris Note outlook of metaphysical despair and mistrust of technical brilliance during the 1930s.

6. According to the recollections of Greta Gerell, as cited by Temira Pachmuss (*Zinaida Hippius: An Intellectual Profile*, p. 395), it was Zlobin who initiated that game of hide-and-seek, concealing himself behind the curtain.

had rented in the Alpes Maritimes in the city of Grasse. Gippius was speaking on the telephone in the vestibule. At first no one paid any attention. But then people began to listen. It was a lively conversation, but it was impossible to say what language she was speaking. Judging by her tone, she was first angry, then polite, then unexpectedly surprised. Then she laughed. When someone went up to the glass telephone booth (just what she had been waiting for), it became clear that she was speaking a nonexistent language. Apparently she used the telephone more than once for her "jokes." One of their regular visitors told me that she bedevilled him over a period of time, calling every evening and claiming she was "Bijou" until, finally guessing who it was, he would hang up.

She was a strange being, almost like someone from another planet. At times she seemed unreal, as often happens with people of very great beauty or excessive ugliness. Brick-red rouge covering her cheeks and dyed red hair which looked like a wig. She dressed elaborately in shawls and furs (she was always cold) in which she would become hopelessly entangled. Her costumes were not always successful and did not always befit her age and rank. She could turn herself into a scarecrow. This looked depressing and it repelled people. Later on, in Paris, people got used to her, to her monocle, her voice like a sea bird's, her purplish, death-like face powder and fiery rouge. But in Russia, after all, it was considered bad taste to use makeup and rouge, especially the way she did. No wonder that in St. Petersburg she had the reputation of being almost a Messalina or, at least, of being extremely affected. Filosofov, who knew her well, treated her with caution: what stunt would she pull next? He didn't like her jokes—they reeked of scandal.

Yet how intelligent she was and what a remarkable poet! The general public knew her least of all as a poet. Fame was something Gippius did not seek in the least. She was modest, excessively so:

> . . . I live in myself,
> And if I don't, isn't it all the same
> If someone remembers you,
> Or if you have been long forgotten.

Yes, she was modest and humble, but sometimes her humility was the result of pride. And her jokes were by no means innocent pranks from a surplus of energy, the way children make mischief. No, they had a different origin. The aim of her mystification was to draw attention away from herself. She hid her true face under various disguises so that no one would guess or find out who she was or what she wanted.

There she was in her Petersburg drawing room or her Paris salon, the famous one on the avenue du Colonel Bonnet. Who, looking at this over-rouged, arrogant older woman lazily lighting a thin, perfumed cigarette, at this capricious decadent, could say that she was capable of burying herself alive in the ground the way the schismatics (whom Vasily Rozanov described with such terror and delight in his book *The Dark Visage*) used to while waiting for the Second Coming? Yes, that was what Gippius ultimately revealed herself to be—a frenzied soul.

The highest degree of this frenzy—the Kingdom of the Spirit and the Second Coming—was revealed to her not through the schismatics burying themselves in the ground, but through another heretical sect, the Khlysty

[Flagellants—S. K.]. In her diary for 1893 there is this entry, "I am going to the Kh—ty. After all, I'm registered at the Council." This council is puzzling, for the only council she could be referring to here would be the Petersburg City Council with its watch tower and balloons to signal fires. But what does that council have to do with the Khlysty heresy? Perhaps "I'm going to the Kh—ty" means something else and she registered with the City Council to help with famine relief during the famine on the Volga. But this version could not be true. The entry is dated 1893 and the Volga famine took place much later.[7] Besides, such civic work is not like Gippius. No, the council she spoke of was a special one which I discovered by accident.

In one of the novels of Alexander Amfiteatrov, *The Destroyed Nests*, if I am not mistaken, the satanic council of the Khlysty is mentioned. It was with this council that Gippius was registered. In her book *Lunar Ants* there is a story entitled "Sokatil,"[8] where a Khlysty rite is described with a great deal of inside knowledge. She never said another word about this anywhere else:

> Don't listen to me, it isn't worth it:
> I speak poor words, I lie.
> And if in my heart there is triumphant knowledge,
> I will withhold it from the people.

7. Zlobin is wrong about this date. The famine in the Volga regions, which served as a major gauge of the rise of social conscience in Russia, took place in 1891–1892. This was the famine during which Leo Tolstoy organized a network of emergency soup kitchens. Anton Chekhov gave up all literary activity in order to devote himself to famine relief work, and the twenty-one-year-old Lenin organized a campaign to sabotage the efforts to feed the starving peasants, believing that starvation would force them to rebel.

8. "Sokatil" was not included in *Lunar Ants*.

She could not live for long in that hermetically sealed world: she would suffocate. She needed an escape. She found one by channeling her frenzy elsewhere despite her idea of the trinitarian structure of the world. But nothing good ever came of this: revolution had begun in Russia, followed by the Bolshevik *coup d'état*:

> If the light goes out, I see nothing.
> If man is a beast, I hate him.
> If man is worse than a beast, I kill him.
> If my Russia is ended, I die.

It was as if she really did die, descending into the grave alive, burying herself so that she would be resurrected along with Russia. And perhaps no one awaited that resurrection with such trepidation, no one prayed as fervently for it as she:

> I'll not go from the door,
> Let the night last, let the wind rage.
> I'll knock until I fall,
> I'll knock until Thou givest answer.
>
> I won't give up, nor step aside,
> I'll knock, I'll call Thee without fear:
> Give me back the one I love!
> Raise her from the ashes!
>
> Return her to her Father's roof,
> If she is guilty—grant forgiveness!
> Spread Thy purifying cover
> Over sinful Russia!
>
> And grant to me, your stubborn slave,
> To see her yet among the living.
> Open up. While she is in the grave,
> I will not leave our Father's door.

The fire in my soul is inextinguishable,
I knock, the door hinges shake.
I call to Thee—oh, hurry!
I shout to Thee—oh, don't delay!

But her prayer was not heard. The inextinguishable fire
in her soul grew weaker every year:

In New Flesh

The green reflection in the glass door.
Automobiles hum below.
I don't think about my homeland.
Why should I? They killed her.

You, of course, will reproach me
For this, for not thinking.
But I only wait for three days to pass:
She will be resurrected in new flesh.

And so the three days passed. But Russia, for whose
sake she had buried herself, was not resurrected. A different Russia was being born in which she needed no one
and nothing, nor did anyone need her. And the hour of
parting struck:

Departure

Until death itself . . . Who would have thought?
(A sleigh at the doorstep, wind, snow)
I know, I know. But how could one think
That this is until death? Completely? Forever?

Be silent, be silent, we don't need hope
(Evening, wind, snow, houses . . .)
But who would have thought that there is no hope?
(A sleigh. Evening. Wind. Darkness.)

THREE

Gippius and the Problem of Evil

Is there a solution to the problem of evil? In the abstract philosophical realm—no. In religion, where there is a place for it, evil as a problem does not exist. There is the mystery of evil, and all that can be said of it is that no one has yet managed to fathom it. Those who have tried agree on one thing: evil evades knowledge. It is like sand that slips through your fingers, like water that flows away between them. It is never what it seems and its deeds are as ambiguous as its words. It can even pretend to be goodness. The falsification is sometimes so skillful that one must be a saint to discern it. According to monks who are experienced in this area, the Devil can take on the appearance of any saint, even of Christ Himself (the only form the Devil cannot take is that of the Mother of God). Saint Theresa of Avila told in her autobiography of the tests she resorted to when she had a vision of Christ. In order to be sure it was He and not the Devil, she made what she called an *acte de défi*. It was explained in a footnote what that was. A Russian equivalent of an *acte de défi* is a slightly obscene gesture. And the Devil, seeing it, turns and flees.

I must confess that this method of fighting evil spirits brings out sinful thoughts in me. Why an obscene gesture and not the cross? Since when has the cross lost its power? Moreover, why did Theresa have that mistrust of

visions, that caution, that almost fear? Did she perhaps
sense in Christ's words, when He spoke to her in those
visions, something not quite normal, strange, perhaps
even tempting? And didn't she test this vision in order to
verify that she was seeing and hearing not the Tempter,
but in fact Christ Himself?

But if the words which disconcerted Saint Theresa
were really Christ's, which can hardly be doubted, then
not only can evil pretend to be good, but in different
circumstances good can seem to be evil. And that would
mean that good and evil are relative and all concepts
about them are a hopeless muddle, a dark labyrinth in
which those who come too close to the mystery of evil
will inevitably find themselves.

But the human soul is so constructed that it will
search for the truth in spite of everything, even if the
search threatens it with perdition. And the soul is right,
not only before itself, but before God. The soul is com-
manded to struggle against evil, but everything hides
from it what evil is. What does the soul know of evil's
origins, its nature, its aims? Nothing. A cheap medieval
print about the fall of the angels cannot satisfy modern
man with his new religious consciousness. And what of
the person who has experienced two world wars and a
revolution in a relatively short period of time, or a savage
who has experienced nothing at all—how can they be
forced to fight evil blindly?

And so, poor human reason comes at last to the conclusion, perhaps a false one, but at least logical, that if
evil is surrounded by such an impenetrable mystery,
there must obviously be a reason for this. It is hiding
something from us. Can it be true that "the Devil is not

as black as he is painted?" Hence the conjectures about who he is, the dreams and hopes, the romantic haze that still envelops the image of the fallen angel. Yes, strange as it may seem, although today man encounters the most unambiguous, undisguised evil at almost every step, this image still attracts human hearts with irrepressible force. I note the contradiction, but say nothing because it cannot be explained even with the help of original sin, about which no one knows anything definite either.

"I am the one people love and do not know," Vigny's fallen angel says.[1] Lermontov's Demon says what the evil spirit is supposed to say:

> I am the one no one loves
> The one all living things curse.[2]

Metaphysically, Vigny is more profound and significant than Lermontov. But Lermontov is immeasurably higher as an artist. In Vigny's poem there is much tastelessness and unnecessary window dressing, things from which Lermontov is completely free. But Lermontov has his own shortcomings and vulnerable spots, which are for the most part not even his own but inherent in Christianity and its teachings about good and evil. Lermontov, for all his demonism, was basically a good Christian. With him everything is simple, even too simple—I am speaking on the religious level—oversimplified, smoothed over, and, oddly enough, safe

---

1. "Je suis celui qu'on aime et qu'on ne connait pas." From the second canto of "Éloa ou la soeur des anges" by Alfred de Vigny.

2. This quotation from Lermontov's "The Demon" is also known in Russia through the popular aria from Anton Rubinstein's opera of the same name, based on Lermontov's poem.

and sound. There is nothing unexpected. There are no discoveries. Evil is disgraced, goodness triumphs:

> And the defeated Demon cursed
> His mad dreams.

And what were his dreams?

> I want to make peace with heaven,
> I want to love, I want to pray,
> I want to believe in goodness . . .

Lermontov thought these dreams were mad because they were unrealizable and impossible. But nothing is impossible for love and this the Demon believes:

> And he enters, ready to love,
> With his soul open to goodness,
> And he thinks that the hoped-for time
> For a new life has arrived.

But "the hoped-for time for a new life" has not yet arrived. The Demon's repentance and vows and Tamara's sacrifice are in vain because the time is not yet come. At the moment when the greatest miracle of love and forgiveness is about to come to pass, an angel shall interfere and make an obscene gesture at the Demon. The Demon, having lost everything, shall remain

> Alone in the universe, as before,
> Without hope, without love.

Tamara, however, will be saved:

> She suffered and she loved,
> And Heaven was opened for her love.

But in that triumph of virtue there is the most profound inner hypocrisy. It is astonishing how lightly Lermontov has treated Tamara's love, finding in it nothing but weakness, delusion and sin:

> At a terrible price she redeemed
> Her doubts . . .

What were her doubts? Was it that she doubted whether the Demon was cursed forever, doubted that there was no forgiveness, no mercy for him? But it was precisely these doubts that were the best proof and measure of her love for which the good Christian Lermontov imposed penance on her. If Tamara doubted and did not believe in the Demon's damnation, then it was because she loved, and her sacrifice was a sacrifice in the name of love.

"Know you that we have long awaited her," the Angel carrying Tamara's soul to heaven says to the Demon. But such a heaven would hardly spell bliss for her. It is easier to imagine that for her there is little difference between that extinguished heaven and hell, when the only one she loves is not there, when she is parted from him, when he is in hell. The human soul will never accept such a heaven.

Will the Devil be forgiven? No one can know that for sure—no one is granted such knowledge. It is in the realm of auguries, a matter of conscience and inner religious experience. If Lermontov were asked what he thought awaited the Devil and his angels on the day of the Last Judgment, he would, in all probability, answer instantly, as if at a catechism lesson: "Depart from me, ye cursed, into everlasting fire, prepared for the Devil and his angels."[3]

3. Matthew 25:41.

The Church, meanwhile, when censuring the teachings of Origen on the salvation of the Devil, censured perhaps not the teachings themselves, but their prematurity. Such things do happen. The present attitude of the Catholic Church toward the heresy of Origen is seemingly more tolerant than it was seventeen centuries ago. When in 1953 there appeared in Italy a book by the late Catholic writer Giovanni Papini, *Il Diavolo*, in which he very unambiguously supports Origen, one would have thought that the book would be banned and the author excommunicated from the Church. But neither one nor the other happened. *L'Osservatore romano*, the semi-official organ of the Holy See, restricted itself to an article which put things in their proper perspective, and that was the end of the case.

But Papini was stricken with paralysis. He lost the use of his right side, so he could no longer write. Many people, including himself, if I'm not mistaken, thought that this was his punishment for this illicit attempt to solve the mystery of evil. How much reality there is in this, however, is difficult to establish. In such cases everything depends on elusive personal factors. There are instances of people getting away with far bolder attempts of this kind, such as the attempt of Zinaida Gippius, of which more presently. But the main thing is that Papini did not come all that close to the mystery of evil. Actually, he didn't even touch it, for the true mystery is not in the salvation of the Devil, but in his fall, in *why* he fell and who he really is. That is the real crux.

There have been many conjectures. I will dwell on the conjecture most characteristic of our times, which conceals within itself a drop of that poison which destroys not only individual human souls but whole peoples and civilizations—the conjecture of Gippius. Her book *Lunar Ants* contains a short story "He Is White." In it Gippius discloses her attitude toward the problem of evil. The story begins with an epigraph from Saint John the Damascene, which is an occasion for temptation in itself: "He is not evil, but good, for he was made by the Creator as a most radiant Angel of light, and since he possessed reason, he was free." The whole force of these words for Gippius was concentrated in the word *free*. The entire story grew out of it.

The plot deals with a university student, Fedya, dying of pneumonia and half-delirious, who sees the Devil. At first he looks "very ordinary, with little horns and a pig-like snout." But he matures before Fedya's very eyes, he begins to grow and becomes "beautiful, very beautiful." "Instead of a coarse, mature Devil there sat before him a somber and beautiful being dressed a bit theatrically in a red cape." Then, having changed for a moment ("out of excessive zeal") into a gray, mangy, but strong and fidgety devil with the traditional Dostoevskian "tail of a great Dane," "the Devil started to become human—a tall, well-built, fairly pleasant man with his blond hair brushed back." "A self-assured sleekness and sureness of his own power could be seen in his face." And Fedya noticed that the man was winged.

Fedya understood that this self-assured, imperious man or superman could be more seductive than any demon, than any snivelling imp; but Fedya himself was alien to him, was not tempted by him, nor did he fear him, and therefore he didn't hate him. Besides, all of this was just the Devil's tricks. Ghosts, transformations . . . If the Devil was all those things, then does it mean that he is nothing definite?

But suddenly, with an inexpressible longing, Fedya lifted himself slightly on the pillows. The man was still sitting next to him. But there were no longer any wings. Instead, there was a middle-aged gentleman with glasses, wearing a threadbare frock coat. And he was weak through and through—such long, weak, ape-like arms hung down, and his back was bent over with weakness, and his head hung so weakly on his neck that it seemed he couldn't remain sitting even for a minute longer in the chair. And, of course, he wouldn't move a finger or open his mouth. However, he did open his mouth and mumbled: "I'm doing this for you. I am yours. Only, everyone, please leave me in peace."

Fedya looked with terror into the Devil's face and recognized himself. "It was Fedya himself sitting before him, only old, frighteningly, supremely weak-willed, with his head hanging down."

"Why are you tormenting me? What did I do?" Fedya groaned. "I've been thinking of you all my life. I didn't know what you were like and even now I don't know because you've repeated my own thoughts in front of me, nothing else. And you sit here now like a weak ape, the way I hated and feared you most, and I wanted to struggle with you but hadn't the strength."

"No strength?" the ape asked sluggishly.

"If the strength of hatred gives rise to the strength of battle, then I had it! I had it!" Fedya almost shouted. "And therefore you're lying, sitting there next to me with my own face. You're a liar! You're a ghost, a shadow! Oh, to think and to torment myself all my life and to know nothing about you, only to hate you! May you be damned!"

The Devil nodded and sounded like an echo, "A

shadow . . . a shadow . . . all your life . . . to know nothing . . . all . . ."

"Tell me," Fedya suddenly implored, "Do you really exist or don't you? If you do, what are you? Who are you? Why are you? Why do I hate you? After all, you must have come to me for something."

Fedya no longer could see the Devil clearly. The long arms and head no longer hung down. An indistinct spot shone there and didn't vanish. There was a head and a body, but Fedya couldn't make out what it was turning into. He could only see the strange blue eyes staring at him.

"Don't rush so," the Devil said quietly. Suddenly he leaned forward toward the table (just like someone's hair falling loose) and glanced at Fedya's clock.

"What are you doing?" Fedya shouted.

"I came to tell you."

The misty figure became brighter and brighter. It brightened slowly but steadily. The darkness fell away from him in pieces and disappeared below, revealing a radiant core.

"Will you be forgiven? Are you trying to assure me that you will be forgiven?" Fedya whispered excitedly, sitting up in his bed.

"No. I won't be forgiven. But even if I were, could you, could all of you, really forgive me?"

"No."

"There, you see. That is why there will be no forgiveness. And no forgiveness is needed."

"Who are you? Why are you like that now? Is it you?"

"Yes, it is I. Listen!"

Fedya looked at him fixedly. And calm blue eyes looked back at him.

"Are you listening? We are both creatures, you and I. But I existed before you. The Creator created love and light. When he created men He began to love them. And He said to Himself, 'I want to send them My greatest gift. I want to give them freedom. I want each of them to be truly in My image and likeness so that of his own free will he will move toward goodness and grow toward the light and won't be like a slave accepting goodness submissively because the Lord thinks it fit.' And he called us, the radiant ones, unto Him and said, 'Who among you will willingly cast a shadow on My earth, willingly, for the sake of humanity's freedom and My love? Who wants to be hated and persecuted on earth, never recognized to the end for the sake of the radiance of My light? For if no shadow is cast on the earth, there will be no freedom for men to choose between the light and the shadow. And they will not be like us.'

"Thus He spoke. And I stepped forward and said to Him, 'I will go.'"

Fedya listened and looked fixedly at the radiating face. The speaker continued, "'I will go and cast a shadow on Thy earth. To the end, I will be like a dog stretched out on the road leading to Thee; let everyone kick aside the dog in order to reach Thee and be as free as Thou. I take on myself the full weight of their curses. But, Almighty One, what do I know? Thou alone knowest the strength of mankind. What if I begin to overcome it?'

"I dared say that to Him. The shadow and suffering of humanity was already in me. And he forgave me, a creature, my first doubt for my first suffering and said, 'I Myself will go down to aid the people when their strength wanes. I Myself in the form of My Son will descend to the earth. I will become one of them in freedom and love and I will die like them and will be resurrected, the first among them. You will recognize Me and will be like a shadow around Me. Your suffering will be great and only Mine and humanity's will be greater. I hereby send you, of your own free will, to the earth in dark raiment. Rise toward My throne in white, as you really are. But for them you will be dark until the Day of Justification, and of that day you will know nothing. Go.'

"And I fell to the earth like lightning . . . plunged into the earth like a thunderbolt. I am here. You see me."

Strictly speaking, that was not a conjecture, it was a dream, a dangerous dream. But Gippius apparently did not realize what she was doing because it is *impossible not to love* her White Devil. Not only does one love him, but one ceases to think about God, one forgets Him as something unnecessary. Gippius could hardly have suspected that her dream could lead, if not to outright demonolatry, then to an almost inevitable blurring of God and the Devil, to their slow and imperceptible fusion into one two-headed figure.

Oh, of course people need beings who will unambiguously arouse in them "the sense of goodness,"[4] openly stating that evil is evil. I agree. But where do we find such beings when the absence of criteria for separating good from evil has become the distinguishing trait of our time, the illness of our age? I fully realize that the interplay of light and shadow, even when it is as captivating as in Vigny and Lermontov, is too costly. Indeed! Who

---

4. Paraphrase of a line from Pushkin's poem "The Monument."

knows this better than we, "the children of Russia's terrible years"?[5] But strange and terrible as it may be, that
same interplay of light and shadow is in the Gospels
where almost everything that concerns sacrifice, freedom, and the salvation of the soul is uncertain and ambiguous. Christianity is not at all a calm haven. It is full
of endless contradictions and temptations, the greatest of
which is perhaps Christ Himself. It was not for nothing
that He said: "And blessed is he, whosoever shall not be
offended in me."[6]

In that same collection, *Lunar Ants*, there is another
story by Gippius, "They Are Alike," about the odd similarity between Judas and Christ. "He was black and
bright all over," Gippius described Judas, "and his raiment was almost too bright: it was yellow." (It is interesting that Gippius used the same technique in this
story as Dostoevsky in "The Grand Inquisitor": her
Christ likewise does not utter a single word.) But what is
unexpected in "They Are Alike" is not the juxtaposition
of God and the Devil, which is hardly new, but the inner
connection between them (Gippius does not say what it
consists of) which causes their external similarity, despite the consciously emphasized "reversibility" of their
physical appearances. But no matter how captivating the
image of Christ is, with His unearthly smile, glowing
with that "joyous joy," the invisible black light eclipses
by its power the soft glow of that smile. And so it is
almost always with Gippius: the more decisively she re-

5. Quotation from an untitled poem by Alexander Blok, dedicated to Zinaida Gippius, which begins: "Those born in the obscure
years . . ."

6. Luke 7:23.

fuses to acknowledge temptation, the more resolutely it besieges her.

In her memoir, *Living Portraits,* in the chapter on Vasily Rozanov, who wrote *The Dark Visage,* she recounts:

"I remember his hurried words at the table one evening at our home:·

"'All right, fine, but I just can't believe, one could never believe that Christ was simply a man . . . But that He might be . . . Lord, forgive me.' (He timidly and hurriedly crossed himself) '. . . that He was perhaps Lucifer, the morning star . . . which fell to earth like lightning . . .'"

Fortunately such thoughts did not occur to him often, otherwise he probably would have gone out of his mind, for the human mind cannot bear such things for long. But in that case, it can be understood why the mystery of evil is an inaccessible stronghold:

Because it is guarded by madness.

FOUR

Gippius and Filosofov

In the spring of 1892 Gippius had another of her chronic bouts of bronchitis. Merezhkovsky borrowed the money from his father and took her first to the Riviera, to Nice, and then, when she had improved, to Italy for a short stay.

In Nice, at the residence of Professor Maksim Kovalevsky, the villa Eden Roc, she met a young St. Petersburg University student, Dmitry Vladimirovich Filosofov. He was extraordinarily handsome. But she was enamored of someone else at the time, a doctor (apparently Chigaev), and took no notice of Filosofov. After returning to St. Petersburg they didn't see each other. It was only six years later, in 1898–99, when the Diaghilev circle and the journal *The World of Art* were launched, that their intimacy began.

From the very beginning, however, there was a certain reserve and coldness in Filosofov. Gippius was drawn to him but she kept it secret. He was more interested in Merezhkovsky and his ideas and he avoided her. There was much in her that he didn't like and she sensed it. On December 19, 1900, she noted in her diary ". . . he [Filosofov] doesn't like me, he is wary of me. This wariness of his (it is not fear) is petty, primitive, trivial. For him I am only a decadent lady, a suspicious *intrigante* and he fears me no more than a centipede."

The Merezhkovskys were in the habit of "saving" their friends (from spiritual downfall, of course). Convinced they were doing a good deed, they would even try to save those "lost ones" who didn't want to be saved. Naturally they couldn't be indifferent to Filosofov's fate, since he was under the influence of Diaghilev and his circle. They thought that for a weak-willed person such as Filosofov the atmosphere of that circle must be demoralizing. And so Gippius began to make plans for his salvation, not without the secret hope of taming him. On the same page of her diary where she had just spoken of his indifference to her, she wrote, "I even feel sorry for Filosofov, who lives in such narrow darkness. There (at Diaghilev's) he will be lost, of course. It is all clear to me. I have to do what I can. I had such thoughts . . ." And then she suddenly comes to her senses: "Why am I talking about Filosofov?" But she was playing games. Filosofov began to interest her more and more each day and she had almost no doubts about her success.

But her first attempt to save Filosofov did not yield the desired results. As long as they didn't encroach on his inner freedom, he was their friend and helper. But when the Merezhkovskys' true attitude toward Diaghilev's circle and particularly toward *The World of Art* was made clear and it turned out that they thought Filosofov was not just in a "narrow darkness," but in a cesspool from which they had to drag him out practically by force, Filosofov drew away from them. By the spring of 1902 he began to distance himself from them "in some strange manner," as Gippius put it. "At times he seems surprisingly hostile."

He then moved in with Diaghilev (Diaghilev was his cousin). Merezhkovsky, who was upset by failure, made an attempt to visit Filosofov and to talk things over with him. But Diaghilev—very politely—did not let him in to see Filosofov.

It looked like a complete break. Gippius fretted and composed two epigrams. One on Filosofov which paraphrased Tatiana's answer to Onegin:

> My friends and mother pleaded still
> With tears and sobs. But for poor Lil
> All fates were equal, all the same.
> I am a wife now and you must
> Leave me alone, forget the past.

The other on Diaghilev:

> A single rooster in the henhouse harem.
> The hens all fight for sway over his heart.
> And in a herd there's a Napoleon—he's a ram,
> And Diaghilev's the lord of *World of Art*.

In March of 1903, a month before Pobedonostsev closed the Religious-Philosophical Society, Filosofov went with Diaghilev to Italy. But the obvious thought that the break occurred through her and Merezhkovsky's fault did not enter Gippius's head. "He was, it's true, ill all the time," she noted, not guessing the real reason for Filosofov's infidelity. "But not so ill that his illness could justify his alienation from us and our cause."

Not long before he left, on February 19, 1903, Filosofov sent a reply to a letter from Merezhkovsky, which unfortunately has not survived. In it he explained with characteristic forthrightness his view of their relationship: "You were angry and gave vent to your bad feelings," he wrote. "Then, like a good Christian, you realized that malice would get you nowhere and you began to feign kindness. This is all boring and unconvincing. If I have already perished, then you cannot save me. If I haven't yet perished, then why do you think you hold a monopoly on salvation? Isn't this your greatest vice—your overweening pride?"

But there was something else about the Merezh-kovskys that repelled Filosofov. "If I sometimes abandon you on a day to day basis," he continued, "it's because of my desire to protect my feeling of liking for you. I am fond of both of you and significant moments in my inner life are connected with you. But when I have to deal with your diplomatic editorial correspondence, which shows so unattractively the full depth of your petty writer's ambition that is so easily wounded by any disagreements with your views, or when you begin to sweet talk me with malice in your heart, then I distance myself from you. I don't want to see you in the guise of people who are alien and repugnant to me."

> The earthly ties of people break at times,
> This one seems to have broken altogether.

Judging by their calm, assured tone, those lines, written by Gippius and dated 1903, must have been written after Filosofov had returned to the Merezhkovsky fold, that is, at the very end of 1903. But her earlier feelings were better expressed in the 1902 poem "Diamond," dedicated to Filosofov, where she said, "We thought we had a brother who was Judas."

II

In October of 1903 Gippius received a terrible blow. On the morning of the tenth her mother, whom she greatly loved, died unexpectedly. And

Filosofov suddenly returned. ". . . I remember him close by all the time," she wrote in her book on Merezhkovsky. "It was precisely then that I knew he would never leave us again. Dmitry Sergeevich was very happy about it."

But Filosofov's return did not actually change anything. His duel with Gippius continued. The only difference was that now the battle was fought in the open, at least from Filosofov's side. Gippius, on the other hand, did not reveal her forces all at once. She had great self-control and an exceptionally strong will which was precisely what Filosofov didn't have. He, for his part, was straightforward, simple, and spiritually chaste—the very qualities Gippius totally lacked.

A little more than a year passed. In that time the Merezhkovskys made their second attempt to "save" Filosofov which was just as unsuccessful as the first. Filosofov launched a counterattack. He asked Gippius why she was so sure she was on the side of truth. On November 26, 1904, she answered him. Here is her reply: "The sincerity of your letter astounded me. I couldn't help hesitating before what may contain the truth. And these past days I have thought long and hard about it. The clash is not between you and me, but between two directions. You negate my essence by your very being. What I consider holy, you consider diabolical. What I create, you see as destructive. I don't care *which* of us is right; I care *where* the truth is. And so, I let myself assume that the truth is with you. I honestly and simply believe that it is possible the truth is with you. Then I and everything that I stand for comes from the Devil. This is a problem that must be solved, things cannot be left as they are."

Filosofov could hardly have believed that Gippius could actually, sincerely admit even for a moment that she was wrong. He knew her well enough to understand what she hoped to gain by taking that approach: she required that he willingly and unquestioningly submit to her truth and reject his own. But inasmuch as that truth was Christianity, Gippius was trying to break down an open door. There were no dogmatic disagreements between them. Filosofov from the very beginning accepted the Merezhkovskys' attitude toward Christianity with all the consequences that arose from their attitude. In her book on Merezhkovsky Gippius confirmed this: "He immediately understood Merezhkovsky as a thinker; his ideas could not but captivate him." The clash between Gippius and Filosofov was a purely personal clash, which Gippius, contradicting herself, admitted at the end of her letter. "You understand," she wrote, "I'm not speaking of our incidental divergences, but about the essential tuning of our souls. When that tuning is revealed in me and in you, we clash." But it then turns out that the situation was altogether hopeless: "If I cross over to your 'truth,' I will go further than you and we would scarcely be able to communicate any more.* If I stay with my former beliefs, again we won't be able to communicate, because you with your bent for spinelessness could never make the effort of will and cross to the other side for the sake of truth alone." And as if in a frenzy, she continued: "When we do meet (and provided that I keep to my beliefs) it will *always* be thus or worse, for I will strengthen what seems holy to me, but what in your

*An allusion to those monastic vows which, hard as it is to believe, Gippius threatened to take.

view 'destroys you and breaks you down' and seems to you a 'numbing poison.'"

This alone shows just how sincerely she admitted the possibility of Filosofov's being right. Whatever form their relationship assumed, neither he nor she would back down from the positions they had taken. Filosofov was indeed exceptionally weak-willed and what she said about his nature was basically correct. But he was not at all opposed to "bringing heaven down to earth." He only pointed out the danger of mixing the two orders—the divine and the human—which are not so easily kept separate in actual practice. Gippius, however, played with that danger all the time.

He did not answer her letter. Further discussions apparently took place during personal encounters he often postponed, sending brief notes in pencil like: "Zina, dear, I cannot make it today." He was not angry with Gippius when she was right. He was fully aware of his shortcomings, particularly his spinelessness, and he did not try to seem better than he actually was, at least not in front of the Merezhkovskys. But Gippius's saintly stance gradually wore him down and in the end led to a split in his personality which paralyzed his will almost completely. Here is a typical letter of his—one out of many—in which he admits the weakness that drove him to despair:

"Dear Zina, I don't know what is happening to me. As soon as I am ready to come see you, I start thinking up excuses not to go. It's some kind of fear, a stupid fear. Sunday I went with my sister to a consultation with our parents and yesterday I went to an editorial board meeting of *Brimstone*. That sort of reaction has started to go away, thank God, and at least I have the strength to write this letter. I think it will all pass, but I have felt so much despair because of my weakness. By the way, I'm not feeling well physically.

"I'll try to come tonight. I said try because I'm not yet sure. But as I said, I'm better, thank God. By tomorrow I hope I'll finally get back on the right track and be rid of this keen desire not to see you, that is, not the two of you, who are the only people close to me, but more likely not to see myself. Yours, Dima."

III

At the end of April, 1905, Filosofov went with the Merezhkovskys to the Crimea where they lived together for several weeks. Then Filosofov returned to St. Petersburg while the Merezhkovskys went to Odessa by way of Constantinople.

On May 12, Gippius wrote to Filosofov a lengthy sixteen-page letter from Yalta. There is nothing in it directly concerning their relationship except for a few remarks that show she was just as much in love as she had been. "Dmitry keeps saying," she added in the margin, "how much our trip has given us. I don't say anything, but how much I know!" And on another page, "We went to Ai Nikola. Even though you weren't there I can't say I didn't enjoy myself thoroughly."* But that letter was important in another sense. In it she discussed for the first time her still uncompleted idea of the "trinitarian structure of the world" which was to have such an im-

---

*At Filosofov's suggestion the three of them had changed to the familiar form of address, using *thou* rather than the polite *you*.

mense influence on Merezhkovsky's work and all their subsequent work together. Filosofov also accepted it, but not all at once and not without reservations.

That spring in the Crimea was the calm before the storm. On the return trip an unexpected encounter awaited them in Odessa. Just at that time, a ship with wounded from the war with Japan arrived. Several officers who had been at Port Arthur were quartered at the hotel where the Merezhkovskys were staying. "The things we got to see in their rooms!" Gippius wrote in her book on Merezhkovsky. "And we were left with the impression that these returnees from the fire of battle had become (or still were) mentally unbalanced." Their encounter provided Gippius with the theme of her short story "There Is No Return" (originally called "A Hole in the Head") which was published in her collection *Lunar Ants*.

The Merezhkovskys spent that summer in a little, old, pleasant cottage at the estate of Little Kobrino near Suida along the Warsaw railroad line. They lived there together with Filosofov. In mid-July he planned to visit his family estate of Bogdanovskoe in the province of Pskov for two weeks. He wanted to see his mother, with whom he had something to discuss, and then he was to return to Kobrino. The matter he wanted to discuss was this: the Merezhkovskys had invited him to go abroad with them for one or two years so that the three of them could live together and discover in their closeness new things that would be useful later for their cause and for Russia. There wasn't anything for them to do in Russia in any case. *The World of Art* was no longer being published, the Merezhkovskys' own journal *The New Way* was also coming to an end, and the Religious-Philosophical Society had been closed down. Filosofov wanted to ask his mother's advice concerning the trip and to secure her approval of it.

As usual, he vacillated. He wasn't afraid of life abroad, he was afraid of life under one roof with Gippius. In Yalta he had already begun to understand what sort of feelings she had for him. And in Kobrino there could be no further doubt on that score.

The morning of his departure for Bogdanovskoe, July 15, she suddenly appeared in his room at dawn while everyone else was still sleeping. He rather rudely sent her back to her room. The evening before he had written her a letter which he slipped under her door as he was leaving. This is what it said:

"Zina, understand me, whether I am right or wrong, aware or unaware, etc., etc., the following *fact*, which *is a fact*, remains and there is nothing I can do about it: my memories of our intimacy are physically repulsive to me.

"This is not a matter of asceticism or sin or the eternal shame of sex. This goes beyond all that, it is something absolutely irrational, something *specific*.

"In my previous sexual relations I felt great shame, but a different kind, having nothing in common with this. There has been vivid hatred, anger, a sense of shame for being attracted to the flesh and only to the flesh.

"But now it is just the opposite. Although my spirit, the whole of my being, is awesomely drawn toward you, there has grown in me a kind of hatred for your flesh which is rooted in something physiological. At times it is almost pathological. For example, today you used my cigarette holder and I can no longer use it because it arouses in me a *specific* feeling of disgust. I wouldn't hesitate for a moment to smoke from Dmitry's holder. And before we were intimate that wouldn't have happened at all. But there has arisen between you and me some kind of *fact* that causes me to feel disgust in the highest degree, to feel a purely physical nausea.

"To consider it in its *coarse* aspect, one could say that anyone who is joined to another without sexual attraction must experience this feeling.

"But this is absolutely wrong. That did happen to me once. But then I felt pity. There was no rebellion, just a boundless regret.

"But here my whole being rebels and I feel a keen hatred for your flesh. This is a fact. Now what am I to do?"

She replied that same day in a thirty-two-page tract sent to Bogdanovskoe. Right or wrong, she loved him, and, therefore, in her own eyes she was right, just as Filosofov in his own eyes was right for not loving her. Her love was noumenal and transcendental, and his lack of love was also noumenal and transcendental. Their duel could not end in victory for either, only in defeat for both. But they didn't understand that and continued to struggle.

"Hear me out, Dima," Gippius wrote. "I have cast a shadow over you and over myself and by reflection I have cast a shadow over Dmitry, but I'm not asking either of you for forgiveness. All I need is to remove these shadows if strength and truth will let me. I ask only one thing of you: don't condemn my effort to express this general truth, even if you see that it was a vain attempt and that I was unable to accomplish anything."

This was just what Filosofov did not want to hear. He

was afraid of uniting God with sex. But she would not take his idiosyncrasy into account and tried to explain what someone who is not in love can never understand. She tried to defend her love, "pathetic sparks, fleeting moments of my *sacred* feelings for you . . . It was all in God, from God, through Him. A moment of religious feeling (not only for you, but for God and for nature) touched my spirit and my soul and *my flesh*. You did not condemn me (and how could you?) where God and nature were concerned, but where you were concerned, you unconsciously or consciously suspected *lust*. That was all too natural. A thread of naked, cold lust has always entered into every kind of sensuality, always, from the very first sensual, carnal moment."

And continuing to disregard the horror and disgust that she was inspiring in Filosofov, Gippius formulated the question thus: "I'll say to you: haven't you known, have you never observed the sensuality of conscious faith? Which moves from the All Highest (not toward Him, as with Saint Theresa) and which is all under His gaze? Can there be in *that kind* of sensuality a thread of lust? Even the most slender thread? Even if imperceptible? Can such things be? I don't dare assert anything about myself absolutely. I don't know anything. But it often seemed to me, I felt, that in relation to you and with you I could do and feel only what I could do before Christ, under His gaze, indeed, in His very presence. That is, so that He not only could be present, but absolutely had to be present. This much I do know about myself and about the fleeting moments of the prelude to my love for you: they were, for all of their carnality, transparent, completely open to God's gaze. Everything was before Him, together with Him."

Zinaida Gippius. A turn-of-the-century
photograph inscribed in 1908 to
her friend Amalia Fondaminskaya.
Photo courtesy of Aleksis Rannit.

Dmitry Merezhkovsky and
Zinaida Gippius visiting
the Symbolist poet
Vyacheslav Ivanov
in Rome in 1937.

Photo courtesy of Aleksis Rannit.

Dmitry Filosofov,
Dmitry Merezhkovsky,
Zinaida Gippius, and
Vladimir Zlobin, photographed
in Poland shortly after
their joint escape from
the Soviet Union in 1920.

Zinaida Gippius in her study in Paris, 1940.

IV

At Bogdanovskoe Filosofov did nothing. He lounged in bed until lunch, went to his room after lunch, and his afternoon tea was brought to his room. He was staying in the manager's quarters, far from the manor. He still hadn't spoken to his mother about Paris. He kept postponing his talk with her. It looked as if he might not go.

Gippius's letter had a demoralizing effect on him. The more he thought about it, the less he knew how to answer it. In general he feared his thoughts. What was he to do about them?

Gippius's letter was a sin—such was his first impression. A sin because it was absolutely sinful to root around "in one's own spiritual guts" for thirty-two pages, or at least so it seemed to him. One ought to keep one's own nightmares, like that "lake of ice," to oneself. Under no circumstances should one enlarge on such topics.

He finally answered her on July 22. "I read your letter this morning by the light of the sun with a fresh mind, and was horrified once more. Oh, not by its contents, not by the facts it stated, not by those internal and external events which occasioned this treatise of yours, but by this very 'Oh!'

"And today, by the light of the sun, and with a fresh mind (which of course does not preclude the possibility of thinking otherwise by the light of the sorceress-moon), I firmly maintain: Zina, beware! Beware of the lure of vain theorizing! Especially beware because ultimately, somewhere in the recesses of your soul, this theorizing, these infusions of mental gnats give you pleasure. Oh, I'm not against games of chess, but with you games always turn into a kind of refined bullfight. For you a game without danger and without wounds does not exist.

"You always think you're struggling with the Devil, but alas, I sometimes think you're struggling against God. Or perhaps if not struggling, then you somehow put yourself on an equal footing with Him. This is terribly frightening and I am beginning to hate you. You categorically maintain that you *know* all about yourself, that you know your experiences, for all their carnality, were transparent and could be pierced through by God's gaze. If *you* have such knowledge, then you are either a saint or are possessed, and in any case cannot be a companion to me. No, I have never observed 'the sensuality of conscious faith' and therefore I can neither affirm nor deny that there is a 'thread of lust' in it. You haven't observed it either, but you affirm you have with the power of a prophet. I say that you haven't observed it, because for such observations the Church is indispensable. Only with the Church behind you, with its full power, that is, only with such a touchstone which cannot *deceive*, can one embark on such experiments. Now, however, while undertaking your lonely sorceries, you do not have the right to say you *know*, for who has verified your knowledge? God or the Devil? *I don't know*.

"Zina, I know that my letter is harsh, and it is especially harsh because I am writing it 'by the light of the sun.' But what am I to do—when one fights, one cannot be sweet. And I am fighting in the first place *for myself*, for my secret which I will never betray and for my simplicity."

Filosofov was of course right—from the point of view of the Church. If Gippius had lived in the Middle Ages, she undoubtedly would have been burned at the stake. But even the Church can be mistaken. It erred when it burned Joan of Arc at the stake. Also, the Church not only has the Gospels, the New Testament, but also the Old Testament, the Bible. In the Bible there is circumcision, the idea of which is marriage to God, the flesh-and-blood union of man and God. However one chooses to regard it, the Bible without circumcision is like Christianity without baptism.

There is of course no commandment which would require Filosofov to love Zinaida Gippius and not somebody else. And if he was fighting primarily for himself, that was his sacred right. The only thing he could be reproached for would be that, from the humanitarian point of view, the time he chose to give Gippius her comeuppance was not exactly opportune.

At his estate Filosofov said nothing to his mother about Paris. He decided to write to her from St. Petersburg. But to decide is one thing: to carry it out is another. When, after much exertion, the letter was finally written, it lay there for a long time, and each new day he lacked the courage to mail it. He didn't want to return to Kobrino without an answer from his mother. He had reached a dead end. Things got to such a state that by his own admission he would "drink himself into a stupor and indulge in boorish debauchery till daybreak."

Finally, on August 2, Gippius sent him a telegram. He answered immediately: "Dear friend, you know me and you know that all my troubles come from my lack of will. The reason I've been stuck here so long is my paralysis of will. Your telegram has brought me to my senses. Together with this letter I will send off the letter to my mother, a copy of which is enclosed. I'll arrive on Thursday at 1:05. If I don't arrive, it means that something has happened. Then come and get me."

But he did arrive.

V

Filosofov had long dreamed of a trip abroad. As early as July 1904, he wrote from St. Petersburg to Gippius in Aussee in Austria where she and Merezhkovsky were spending the summer: "Yesterday Chulkov[1] and I were making plans. We thought of emigrating and publishing a journal abroad. He, of course, wants this for political reasons and I for religious ones. It was so nice to daydream and those plans are still on my mind. We are concerned that our external lives should correspond more closely to our internal lives. I think the most practical thing would be to make the internal departure at the same time as the external departure. For me that departure is very difficult. A heroic feat. But it would be a feat with results."

The future appeared to Filosofov in rosy hues, which was at the very least surprising for such a cautious skeptic as he. "And suddenly there will come a day and an hour," he dreamed, "when we will say to ourselves: Now we are strong. Let us return to our homeland. We will say we left for their sake so that we could return to them strong, healthy, wealthy, that we thought of them constantly because we have much love. God bless our endeavor!" Of himself he wrote, "If that is to be, we must

1. Georgy Chulkov, the Symbolist writer and critic, originator of the theory of "Mystical Anarchism."

prepare gradually, with compassion for *me*, not endlessly reproaching me for my weaknesses (I myself know them), pitying me, not merely loving me."

In the letter to his mother, dated August 2, 1905, in which he asked for her blessing for his "new life," he wrote in approximately the same manner about his trip: "You've known for a long time that I have been extremely dissatisfied with myself, that my life has somehow turned out in such a way that my words do not correspond to my actions. And now, finally, I've decided to make a complete change." That meant breaking with Diaghilev. "You have reproached me more than once," he wrote in the same letter, "for having parted ways with *The World of Art* and for going over to the enemy camp, while at the same time you imply that you fear I have done so under the harmful influence of Z. N. [Zinaida Nikolaevna—S. K.]. It is hard for me to give you all the details, nor is it necessary. I will only say that my path has diverged from Seryozha's [i.e., Diaghilev's—S. K.], and in order to prevent our intellectual differences from turning into hostility because of our day-to-day closeness, I have to spend some time away from him and away from *The World of Art*."

Filosofov did not deny Gippius's "harmful influence." But he did deny his romance with her. "I know, dearest, everything that is being said about my relationship with Z. N. I know that without having an exceptional confidence in me one would be hard put to give up the idea that I'm in love or that 'dear little Zina has sunk her claws into me,' and so on. Here I count not only on your maternal insight, but also on your love and your confidence in me. I have no proof to offer that would convince you. All that is needed is faith. If that is difficult for you now, then, dearest, I beg you on my knees to believe me, if only for a while, for the time being. Soon, soon God will grant that you be convinced I was right and that you not regret your faith in me."

But "maternal insight" was just what Anna Pavlovna did not have. She did not sense that her Dima was not in love with Gippius. In her reply of August 4 from Bogdanovskoe she wrote: "You will not make me change my mind about dear little Zina having sunk her claws into you. But this proves nothing. I will be totally frank and will tell you sincerely once and for all and *for the last time* everything that I think about dear little Zina and then let's drop the subject, shall we?

"You are spineless, and thank God that it is Zina who has you in her clutches, and not some courtesan along the lines of Elizaveta Nikolaevna or Vera Muravyova. She is intelligent and will give you *intelligence*. As for the carnal ecstasies she lavishes on her *base* admirers, of which they so cynically brag, please try to understand that this does not concern me.[2] What business is it of mine? Personally I dislike her, because she is affected, but she and I have no bones to pick with one another. She means nothing to me and she can forget that I exist, for all I care. It is not for the likes of her to come between your heart and mine."

2. The provocative manner of dress that Gippius affected and her use of makeup, in conjunction with her reputation as a "decadent" poet, made the people of Anna Filosofova's generation regard her as a Messalina. Filosofova's feminism, based on the ideals of the Age of the Great Reforms (the 1860s), made no allowances for sexual liberation of women. Feminists of her generation were in fact horrified by the new strain of sexual frankness that characterized early Russian Symbolism.

She gave him her maternal blessing at the very beginning of the letter: "You know that you will always have
my blessing wherever you are and for as long as I live.
I'm very sorry you did not bring this matter up earlier. It
is not news to me." Filosofov had written to her the previous fall about his plans for life abroad (when he was
daydreaming with Chulkov). Anna Pavlovna reminded
him that he had: "Ask Zika* how sympathetic I was to
your trip. I said that no matter how hard it was on me, it
was my duty to accept it for your sake and for the sake of
your future. I don't believe that you people could reveal
more to the world than the 'Herzens and people like that'
have, you have less talent, but I would be thankful for
whatever you can reveal."

After such a letter Filosofov could have gone off with a
clear conscience, the more so because Anna Pavlovna was
taking care of the financial aspect of the trip. But he
suddenly fell into the same mood that preceded his break
with the Merezhkovskys in 1902. The situation became
even more complicated because Gippius, too, began to
lose heart. If she hadn't gotten hold of herself in time,
Filosofov might have broken with the Merezhkovskys
completely on this occasion.

VI

Six weeks after Anna Pavlovna's letter, on September 13, Gippius wrote to Filosofov: "The thing is, I
don't believe in us. This is terribly frightening. I am
hardly able to live through this alone, but I must. The

*Zinaida Vladimirovna Ratkova-Rozhnova, his sister.

two of you don't help me, you don't support me, because you can't. If you could, then I would have believed.

"Basically I don't believe that we will accomplish anything by our union. None of us has the strength for a union. Any old-fashioned relationship is closer than ours, more solid, *more real*. We are capable of neither the old ways nor the new.

"Dmitry is such that he doesn't see another's soul; it holds no interest for him. He isn't even interested in his own. He is alone, without suffering, inherently and by his very nature alone. He doesn't even understand that this can cause torment. You seem spellbound, in a phenomenal paralysis. You are a cry in a dream when there is no voice, your impotence is exceptional in its manifestation, the walls of your home are fireproof. It could be that you suffer because of that—I don't know. I don't care, because if you do suffer, it doesn't show, it isn't revealed, it doesn't concern the world, it is as if it weren't there. There is no path to you or from you.

"I am worst of all. And I feel worst of all. I took the vivid feelings I experienced (where did they come from?) for facts. I pretended 'let this chair be a carriage and that one a horse,' and off we would go. I saw it all that way and felt as if I were going somewhere.

"I am a petty, self-serving, lecherous, and cold soul. And all that business about the 'burning cold' is a pose. An *ordinary*, cold, rather dry, selfish female soul with a knack for deceiving myself when it comes to arranging my little pleasures.

"I have never loved you and never was in love with you, and all that was only my hysterical self-deception. Perhaps I didn't even ever pray to God. All that too was a deception of *desires*, but a dry soul cannot be moved.

"After all, I no longer pray now. I'm not even interested in anything connected with religion. I don't love you a bit and I can't even imagine what it was like when I wanted it and thought it was there. The house has been thoroughly swept."

Gippius was right, of course. But that was only part of the truth. Otherwise the only thing left for them, for the three of them, to do would be to go their separate ways. Filosofov understood that and they continued to correspond. Three weeks later Gippius sent him another letter which could have been written by a different person. For sixteen pages she developed the theme of the dangers of living a "double life." Typical of that letter were lines that seemingly had no direct bearing on the topic: "He who is loved more than he loves is under the power and in the hands of those who love him. What actually happens is what should not happen—the human power of one person over another. The trampling of freedom."

It had apparently dawned on Gippius that the only possible way of saving her relationship with Filosofov was not to infringe on his freedom: live as you wish, choose whatever you want. And on the night of October 9 (the anniversary of her mother's death), she wrote to him, "Several days ago (before you and Berdyaev[3] came to see us) I suddenly, for no reason, clearly and with certainty imagined your coming to us and saying, with torment bordering on hostility, that you could neither be with us nor travel with us, that there were complicated reasons, etc. I even knew how I would answer you: by saying almost nothing. By saying much less than I did in

3. Nikolai Berdyaev, the noted philosopher and a frequent literary associate of Merezhkovsky and Gippius.

1902. I answered that you should do what you can and want to do, that we would stay and wait for you, that you would always, at any time, find us the same as when you left, and that we believed you would come back. And that is all, none of it is new, you've known it for a long time. It is unshakable."

That was very intelligent of her. But she should have stopped right there. Then Filosofov would almost certainly not have done what she was prompting him to do. But she did not stay within the boundaries and the results turned out to be the opposite of what she had wanted.

"And that 'dream of imagination' haunted me with astonishing, concrete clarity," she went on. "Later on, that 'dream' seemed to me to be unrealizable. You don't have the courage (or do you?) simply to come to us soon and say it to us of your own volition. You wouldn't be able to make up your mind and later you probably would write us a letter. But not very soon. In any case, I *sense* that you *don't want* to go or maybe you *want* not to go. But it is tormenting that you love us less than we love you, and so you *don't dare* tell us that openly, to our faces (as you should!) and you almost don't dare to accept my help which I *so* want to give you."

The last statement is rather dubious. Gippius's "hallucinations" (as she called them) would not liberate Filosofov; on the contrary, they would entangle him, and surely such "trampling of freedom" could only outrage him. He felt more and more like a rabbit facing a boa constrictor. Although Gippius acted without conscious calculation, her actions automatically led to the rabbit being swallowed. And then, a surprise. The rabbit was resisting.

VII

What the Merezhkovskys received was not a letter, but a memorandum on five legal-size pages and without a salutation. "I am not going to Paris (it is not, of course, a question of the actual trip, but of its symbolism), because I sense a kind of violation of the equilibrium of our trinity." The violation was that Filosofov had suddenly become bored. "If I had not said 'I am bored,' I might have gone, because the equilibrium would not have been upset. But why did I say 'I am bored'? You maintain that it is because of my inner weakness. *I believe you*. I do believe you, but I myself do not see it with complete clarity. I think that there were many external factors. But since you have doubts, I also have them, and therefore I give in without any hysteria, without passivity, but simply and joyfully."

Once Filosofov had reproached Gippius for her love of "infusions of mental gnats." But he was no better than she, as can be seen from his disquisition on boredom. Gippius was right; he desperately wanted not to go to Paris and was glad for any excuse to get out of the trip. "But thinking about this," he continued, "I have to say that our trinity was not only violated by my weakness, but also by the fact that in my moments of strength Zina intensified our personal relations too much. In spite of all my faith in her as a part of the whole, I have the feeling that she is experimenting on me. That is, she is unconsciously making me not the goal, but the means, and is staging experiments that are *dangerous*. The feeling doesn't leave me for a moment that she is practicing *sorcery* on me, that I have gotten entangled in the innumerable strands of Zina's *personal* spider web. I demand that

Zina totally give up on the relationship she wants from me. Perhaps temporarily, until our equilibrium is reestablished, perhaps even forever. But so long as I sense that things are muddled and confused, while I sense the use of *sorcery* here, she has no right to disregard my feelings, because this is a form of rape."

The rabbit's ultimatum was accepted. Complaints against the boa constrictor ceased. But a short time later the rabbit itself scrambled right into the boa's jaws.

Filosofov took Gippius out to dinner at Donon's. There they unexpectedly ran into Diaghilev, who made a violent scene. That was at the end of December, just before Christmas. "The incident with Seryozha," Filosofov wrote to Gippius, "has had the most serious consequences. He wrote to my mother, asking her to forgive him, but he can no longer visit our house because for *personal* reasons, not on *principle*, he can have nothing further to do with me. While I was still doing everything in my power so that we could part on matters of principle, I couldn't bring it off. But with the first petty, filthy, personal incident which for me *personally* is *filth*, Seryozha found it possible to drop me completely." But there was even more important news in his letter: "Mama in passing said to me today that she wants to consult Dr. Chigaev and then, after Zika leaves, to talk to me *seriously* about our affairs. She wants to know if she should give up the apartment and go abroad in April to stay with my sisters. She herself broached the subject! It will all come to pass!"

At last the day of departure was set. Filosofov was to leave first, on February 10. He would accompany his mother to Switzerland to see his sisters, and from there go to Paris, where he would meet the Merezhkovskys.

They were planning to leave ten days after he did and to arrive in Paris on the same day as he, or at least on the following day. On the eve of his departure Gippius sent him a farewell letter: "My joy, my baby, go with God's blessing. My love will follow you. Christ will strengthen my miraculous love and will strengthen you and keep you safe. He Himself is with you. He Himself will preserve you for Himself, for me and for us."

It is touching. It is only a pity that behind God there lurked a boa constrictor.

VIII

Filosofov was to leave from the Warsaw Station at 12:00 noon. At 11:00 Diaghilev arrived at the Nikolaevsky Station from Moscow. He learned of Filosofov's departure plans from Ratkov-Rozhnov who had met him at the train and he rushed over to the Warsaw Station. In his letter from Berlin Filosofov described their encounter. "Seryozha arrived five minutes before the train left. We kissed each other warmly. It was hard for me, terribly hard. Pity for him flooded my heart and I felt frightened. And in general I feel terrible. God, how will everything turn out?"

Gippius answered him, "Yesterday Berdyaev came and started telling us about seeing you off. He said your face looked sad. And suddenly I became bored, so bored that I still am. At first, for two whole days, I felt radiant, cheerful and calm. Good." In the margin she added, "How was it when Seryozha saw you off? Was it nice? And for him? And in general?" She also added, "I don't quite know what I want—whether I want you to be in

Paris soon or not so soon. Probably the first because of my new fears."

In that letter the Devil appeared for the first time—one of the leading actors in the daily drama of Gippius's life. He was to play a role in her relationship with Filosofov. At first he was shy and only got in their way as they packed: "There are temptations all around, the Devil keeps butting in constantly. I had just begun to sort out our papers when I burned an important document which was lent to me for one day by Serafima Pavlovna [Remizova—S. K.].[4] Dmitry is experiencing unheard of temptations from Moscow. I would like to leave no later than the nineteenth or the twentieth. The Devil gets in the way everywhere, it's gotten so that I am afraid of everything."

In the next letter, which she mailed without knowing for certain whether Filosofov was in Frankfurt or Geneva, she wrote: "Dima, my dearest, I'm so cold, so very cold. That you *are there* and are as you should be is the only thing that gives me support. Your letter made me so happy. But all the same I'm cold." This coldness was also from the Devil, from the "lake of ice." When she received a telegram from Filosofov about his departure for Paris, she warned him: "I beg of you, *don't start* anything in Paris without us, don't form any relationships with people, not even the most casual ones. This is very important and it will help my internal state."

In Paris they stayed in the Hôtel Iéna, place Iéna, but not for long. They quickly found an empty apartment in

4. The wife of the writer Alexei Remizov and a noted paleographer in her own right. As the diaries of Gippius indicate, Serafima Remizova was emotionally drawn to her in ways Gippius was not able to reciprocate.

a new building in Auteuil at 15 bis, avenue Théophile
Gautier. They moved their belongings in and then left
for the Riviera, first to St. Raphael, then to Cannes
where they stayed at the Hôtel de l'Esterel on the route de
Fréjus, on the road to La Bocca.

Filosofov had room No. 17. On April 11 Gippius sent
him a letter through the porter which showed that her
sorcery was not in vain. "Know, believe, or, if you already know, then always remember that everything that
happened was *absolutely necessary* for us both." But her
victory was illusory and she sensed it: "Darkness was
never so close as it might be now. Dark depression, dark
loneliness, dark spite . . . Dima! There can be no truth
in them." And she pleaded: "Don't sin with depression,
with hate or with regret. I feel radiant."

At the end of April Filosofov returned to Paris several
days earlier than the Merezhkovskys in order to get the
apartment ready for their arrival. On April 29, the evening before their departure, Gippius sent him an eigh-
teen-page treatise to the Hôtel du Louvre where he was
staying. Almost all of it was devoted to describing a
conversation with the Devil. "The abyss of our frailty,"
she wrote, "is becoming more and more apparent to us.
It is revealed to us by the abyss of our fear. Truly, fear is
the beginning of wisdom. Because one must know how
frail one is. I'll tell you (I've said it before, but I can't
help repeating it) that the torment of fear in me has been
so great that at times it has clouded everything. It was all
I saw and I could no more take my inner gaze away from
it than you could from an enemy ready to pounce on you
the moment you turned your back. And do you think
that I cannot see right near me the grimacing face of the
Devil? He kept repeating to me over and over until he

grew tired: 'You do not love him, you do not love him, don't be comical, don't deceive yourself. Where is the firmness of your consciousness? Have the courage and the honesty to admit, if only to yourself and to me, that you do not love him and are not even enamored. It's your imagination, your stubborn head, your self-training. Honestly, you aren't even enamored. It was just a bit of lustful passion and not even much of that—remember, there used to be more of it. Please note that your lust is stronger in his absence, so it is all in your imagination. Real infatuation, real passion are quite different. You are irritated by his resistance, you are being stubborn, power-mad, it is all in your imagination. You do not love him and you are not enamored. Don't deceive yourself and me.' That's what he kept saying until he grew tired. But he did grow tired. By myself, all alone, with my strength alone I couldn't have withstood him. After all, he isn't any less intelligent than I, his consciousness is equal to mine. But I kept turning to the other side and there I found the strength to move somewhere above and beyond consciousness (it *alone*) into the realm of some unshadowed truth and from there I could answer him. 'No, I do love him. That's how I want it. This isn't by my will or by yours. I and He, not I and you.' And the Devil changed the look on his face. He then said to me: 'Well, what of it? Now do you see? Is there much joy in what you have attained? How much passion did you get out of it? Weren't your dreams, your imagination more blissful than reality? You have a hot head, but an average temperament. You wanted experience—there's experience for you. That was reckless of you, very reckless. Even speaking from your romantic point of view, wasn't it really more fun, more enigmatic, more intoxicating, more exhilarating, more fiery before you had those two or three nights? There is the tremble of uncertainty, the blessed tremble of the freedom of the *not quite yet.* Not quite reaching the possible—now that is the freedom to suppose that complete happiness lies in what is possible, as well as in what was and what can happen. It depends on you, a human being: stretch out your hand and grasp it. You are always free to think that if you do not grasp it, it is because you *yourself* didn't want to. That is also a kind of happiness. But what about now? Isn't it clear that you can't do anything? You have only lost the intoxication of human possibility. It was reckless in still another way. You do not "love," but I'll allow that you may need this person, that he is somehow necessary to you, perhaps even physically. Why did you not use your judgment and try to bind him to you by sex, purely by passion? There is no argument at all that he doesn't love you. But if you could have controlled yourself and your consciousness, even when you were powerless over your passion, you could have tied that loose thread and grasped the end of the chain that now dangles free and does not fetter him. What were you thinking about? It is all so unintelligent! To teach you so many things for so long, only to see you lose everything in your moment of need because you were paralyzed by your utopian "respect for the rights of the individual," your imagined "love," and your absurd fear which comes from I know not where, surely not from me and not from anything human. Just think what you could have accomplished, compared to what you have now, had you been more intelligent, simply more intelligent.'

"That is what the Devil told me. But I knew it was he. You have to realize, Dima, that it was the Devil. I am writing all this to you on purpose. I don't want to be afraid. I want to be at your side while struggling against him. I've struggled too long alone (here). And you are still alone with your own Devil. But I believe, I can see that you will vanquish your Devil, just as I will vanquish mine, and I believe that mine will not frighten you. Perhaps they (yours and mine) will turn out to be the same. Then we will be two against one. Victory will not be more certain, but the struggle will be easier."

IX

Filosofov did not have the time to answer this letter because two days later, on May 1, the Merezhkovskys were in Paris, at the apartment he had prepared for them. But then, what could he have answered? That the sorcery continued? That great violence was being perpetrated on his person, that he didn't dare say or even think that he didn't love her, that is, didn't love her the way she wanted because that would be the work of the Devil, that she had both God and the Devil at her beck and call, passing off what is God's work for the Devil's and what is the Devil's work for that of God? That there were moments when he wanted to drop everything and get on a train not even for St. Petersburg, but for Bogdanovskoe? That if he weren't ashamed, he would certainly have done so? Every time he managed to get away by himself, even for a day, was a respite. It was restful just to walk around Paris by himself.

At the end of the summer the Merezhkovskys went to Pierrefonds. Filosofov came with them. He was there until October 8 and then he set off for Amiens for a few days at a congress of syndicalists. He sent Gippius three postcards. She answered with a short letter expressing her regret over his absence. "Somehow it isn't right without you. I need you every minute of my life, in every way and in every situation. Sometimes I need you at a distance, but not too far away and for no longer than six or eight hours. Don't forget that you promised to tell me absolutely everything about the congress, about its significance, what you do outside of it, about you and about everything."

Filosofov wrote very little about the congress, mainly that "two emotions prevailed there: envy (the reformers, concerned with affluence, the kind that the bourgeoisie has) and hatred (the anarchists)." He asked the Merezhkovskys to send him fifty francs by registered letter, just in case, because he was afraid he didn't have enough money.

Gippius asked him, not without sarcasm: "Admit it, you're happy being free, aren't you? Never mind, never mind. It's an illusion. You aren't 'free' because, after all, I still love you." That was all the more unexpected because two days earlier she had encouraged him: "Enjoy yourself to your heart's content, make use of every hour. In Paris you won't be able to hop around at will."

Filosofov planned to return and he let the Merezhkovskys know when he would be arriving. But the congress dragged on and he decided to stay another day. By way of an answer Gippius, who had in the meantime returned from Pierrefonds to Paris with Merezhkovsky, gave him a sharp scolding. In miniscule handwriting she wrote on a postcard: "The point is not that Nouvel*

*Walter Nouvel, a high school friend of Filosofov and a friend of and assistant to Diaghilev, who was at that time in Paris.

might be right in saying that you bring your old way of thinking to your enthusiasm for civic concerns, or that you are still enthusiastic about some old way of thinking or other. The point is that your old way of thinking, which is *a lack of responsibility* for your actions and a refusal, for whatever reason, to do what you yourself freely advocate, seems to me the greatest danger of all. As we see it, you should have long since changed your old way of thinking. That trivial fact hurts me deeply *for your sake*. I must assume that it was your *lack of responsibility* for yourself, because I cannot believe that you were already thinking of staying when you asked us to send you the fifty francs. You asked for it just in case, so that you wouldn't worry. Forgive me if you don't like this card, but I have to be honest. And *that* old way of thinking is equally unacceptable in small matters as well as large. I have to admit that *neither* of us liked this at all."

"If anyone has the old way of thinking," Filosofov answered her, "then it is you, and I categorically protest against it. I had already packed, in order to return today in time for dinner. But when I saw in your rude letter the use of force, which I find intolerable, I decided on principle to stay to the *end* of the congress and will not return until tomorrow. You weren't even ashamed to say something as vile as that I lied when I asked for the fifty francs. You should be ashamed."

Perhaps she was ashamed, but when she was overcome with jealousy she lost her head. Nor did Nouvel, whom she had invited to dinner, bring her any comfort. She learned from him that Diaghilev was in Paris with an exhibition of *The World of Art* painters. She was afraid Filosofov would see him, feared his "old way of thinking." Filosofov, who was also afraid of seeing Diaghilev, wrote to her from Amiens: "After all, his [Diaghilev's] territory is very limited* and you and I can go quite safely to the Left Bank. While I have so much to do and I am in this mood, it won't be a deprivation for me to avoid the Boulevards." But besides Diaghilev, whom he managed to avoid, there were other temptations stalking Filosofov, as can be seen from Gippius's letter of October 1907. What they were, however, and whether he managed to resist them is not known. But when Diaghilev came to Paris the following year with a series of Russian concerts, Filosofov "fell." He went to the concerts and visited Diaghilev in his room at the Hôtel Hollande. Gippius wrote to Filosofov: "I feel immersed in an absurd, meaningless chaos of life and of days which pass under the smile of a petty devil. I was obsessed during the night, as if someone were whispering it in my ear that the Devil was tempting you, not even going to the trouble of thinking up something new, like revolution, but tempting you with the same old tailcoat. He doesn't even tempt you into sin, but simply into drawing away from the cause of our lives, into moodiness, cowardly sluggishness, a muddy rut. And it frightens me that just a year ago he tried to ensnare you more slyly and cleverly, but failed. Yet now there's the tailcoat, and the music is good, and instead of me there's Nouvel sitting next to you, and you're in the mood and everything is so simple and natural and nice and good. So how can there be any possible objections?"

It is amazing that such an undoubtedly intelligent woman as Gippius did not know how to handle people. She drove Filosofov to the point where he couldn't listen

*He was staying at the Hôtel Scribe near the grands boulevards.

to her without getting irritated. "Your presence paralyzes me now," she wrote to him at the end of 1907. "I can't speak when I *know* that I must. That, of course, is not my fault and I don't care whose fault it is. Words that I write to you are more acceptable and I will give in to that weakness today." And she summed up their life together for the past year. "Let's not bother deceiving ourselves. We *know* too deeply that you cannot enter a new life with either the old way of thinking or with the old physiology, or with the old way of life. When we are drawn to a new life, we *naturally* have to restructure both our life and our way of thinking and that is not a path strewn with roses. Nor is it all roses restructuring our physiology, which is also inevitable. Your tone implies that you could manage all that if it weren't for the circumstances. It's not ideal, but it's not really bad. You yourself know that this is nonsense."

Then she made a confession which she was later to retract: "We don't want to suffer. But what we want cannot be attained without the greatest suffering. Otherwise, not a step can be taken." Let us be fair: love has caused few people as much suffering as it caused her. Why was it, then, that she gained nothing by it and lost everything?

X

People are amazing creatures. Give them the freedom of choice in love and, with rare exceptions, they will choose, out of a thousand, the one person who will cause them the most suffering. Filosofov was just such a person for Gippius.

The final break between them occurred at the end of 1919 in emigration, when the Merezhkovskys left Warsaw for Paris on the day the Riga Conference began, while Filosofov remained in Warsaw with Savinkov to continue the fight against the Bolsheviks. But internal disagreements had occurred long before. A rift had formed even before World War I and perhaps there had never really been total harmony. But they continued to correspond and to meet even after the break. When Filosofov was in Paris on business he would see the Merezhkovskys even though there was little joy in those visits either for him or for them.

At the end of January 1913 Gippius wrote from Menton to Filosofov in St. Petersburg: "Dima, my precious, my beloved, my sweet joy, please come to me! I beg you, with all my heart and soul. I have never yet begged like this before. My heart is pointed toward you like an arrow. Come here. If for some reason you can't, then come for my sake alone. I know, you'll see, how important and good that will be for our whole *future*. My dearest, if you should want, I'll come to you some other time. I would come now to St. Petersburg, but you would misunderstand it (you'd think I was coming to get you). Just call me and I'll come. But that is not the point. Please try to understand me, even if it takes a miracle; try to understand how important it is for the sake of Christ. My soul aches terribly. Help me; all my love is for you; don't hesitate, don't judge me. I'm not deceiving you, I'm not exaggerating, I won't even say anything, I only implore you, call to you, scream for you.

"God will help us; you will hear me. Please come *now* and then leave when you want. Stay as long as you want with whomever you want. I will count the days. Send a telegram when you get this. (And if you can't come *quickly*, then don't answer at all.) But I believe you will understand. How could you not understand? I love you so deeply and I beg of you unceasingly to come. I know what it is for me, what it means for me and for everyone.

"My joy, I am waiting for you and will be forever beholden to you for this. And you will not regret it."

The next day she sent a second letter after the first. "Dima, my dear, I have sent you a letter and I won't recant or take back one word of it. But I got to feeling sorry for you. Such a request may seem to violate your freedom. No, I want you to be free. But I also want to be totally candid. You know me, you know how difficult it is for me to be candid and beg. But it is better for me like this. Don't be afraid to offend me and don't be afraid to refuse. Don't torment yourself over anything. You will understand, you are sure to understand, and if you still do not come, it will mean that you don't think it would be good for you. I'll also say sincerely that in my desire for you to come there are again two interlaced threads, a personal one and one pertaining to our cause. I want you to know that. Because of it, my desire is deeper and keener, but perhaps for you it is less valid. Know everything and act freely. Again I say that I take complete responsibility for every word and each stands as it is, regardless of your reply to my request, regardless of what you might freely decide to do.

"I simply wrote you yesterday, having forgotten a lot of things, having forgotten the complexity that has be-clouded us all. I must have been thinking about Zina [Zinaida Ratkova-Rozhnova, Filosofov's sister], who summoned you from Cannes to St. Petersburg, or about something along those lines. I was thinking mostly of your help. Everything remains as it was, I only want to make you feel completely at ease and completely free, and not because of my pride, but *only out of love*. I can't possibly say more and as God is my witness I have told only the truth. If you don't come it means that for you it is just as important and necessary that you *do not come* as it is for me to have you here."

Filosofov did not reply at once. Gippius, thinking he wasn't coming, wrote to her sister Tatiana in St. Petersburg several days later: "It was *not* that Dima didn't come because of the collection of essays. He knew he was needed here, *he knew that*. Such are the facts. But he has a physical need to live without *us*, to live his own life. This is invincible by anything, even our common cause. He has two feelings of ill will, one toward me and the other toward Dmitry. They are different, but of the same intensity. I not only do not blame him, but I don't even deny that for all that he in some way loves us. Slowly and steadily his hatred is growing and his love is correspondingly dwindling. It is hatred, or more likely the inability to stand us, call it what you will. I repeat that I don't blame him one bit, he isn't happy about it himself. But I had to see clearly and definitely the limit to which his hostility could rise, to understand fully the limit beyond which it is no longer possible to continue our so-called relationship. For this, I exposed all the *pretexts*. Besides that, without politics and polemics and with only all my love, I indicated to him clearly every possible path of return. I asked him to come back when he chooses, how he chooses and for whatever reason he chooses. I gave him at once everything I had—faith and love and freedom. That was a necessary sign and I can accept calmly what followed. I don't regret that I gave him everything, but I can finally see that I have nothing more to give him and that he in fact no longer needs me. Everything has changed between us, but before myself and before God I can now say that if that change is wrong, then I had no hand in it."

Filosofov did, however, come back. He came, but nothing changed. His ill will toward the Merezhkovskys continued to grow. Gippius explained it by his illness: "In the spring, after a winter filled with activity and hard work, we went to Paris and then to Menton," she wrote in her memoirs. "I went with Merezhkovsky, because Filosofov had to finish some family business and, besides, he was in a dismal mood. This was soon explained by a decline in his health—a painful liver ailment. When we learned of this in Menton, Merezhkovsky and I summoned him to join us as soon as possible, and he came. At first his attacks continued, but then he began to recover and with his recovery his state of mind also improved."

But it was only a brief respite.

XI

There had been times in the past when Filosofov hated the Merezhkovskys. But hatred never completely filled his heart. It would flare up and then die down. Only after the death of his mother in the spring of 1912 did the Merezhkovskys become "unbearable" for him. In the same letter from Menton to her sister Gippius wrote: "Only with death in one's heart can one hate the living the way Dima, clinging to the grave, recoils from us."

The situation was also complicated by the fact that Filosofov had moved in with the Merezhkovskys after their return to Russia from France in May 1908. At first they lived in the famous Muruzi House in Liteyny Prospect, then in a house across from the Tauride Gardens at 83 Sergeyevskaya Street. Certainly he loved them "in his own way," as Gippius wrote, otherwise life together would have been unthinkable. But he had his own work, his own interests, and he tried to avoid arguments, considering them pointless. Still, it occurred often enough that literally everything about the Merezhkovskys annoyed him. Then the arguments would take an ugly turn and lead to innuendoes. In her memoirs, written soon after Filosofov's death and not long before her own, Gippius summarized his character, trying to be as objective as she could: "He was very tall, well-built and incredibly handsome. All of him, down to the tips of his elegant fingers, seemed to have been born to become an aesthete. His aristocratic manners were not at all like Diaghilev's and betrayed his capricious, stubborn, and inactive character and at times an attitude akin to contempt. He had genuine depth, but unfortunately he was always unsure of himself and tended to underestimate his powers in any given area. He possessed real culture and was well educated, but he lacked confidence in his writing ability, although he could write articles that were bold and pointed. He was religious, *not superficially* but by nature, and in this area he was very chaste. But the background of Dmitry Filosofov's soul was for the most part gloomy and pessimistic, and at the end of his life there appeared in him something embittered and hardened.

"He was closer to Merezhkovsky than to me and he surely loved him more than he loved me. He always treated me with mistrust. He mistrusted my 'pranks,' for which, however, Merezhkovsky often assumed responsibility. Even now, however, I do not doubt," she concluded, "that he sincerely loved Merezhkovsky and even both of us, just as we loved him. During fifteen years of living together I had become sure of that."

That was the "official" version. We know how it really was. Her poems are closer to the truth. The first poem dedicated to Filosofov was called "The Limit." It is dated 1901 and belongs to the period of "pre-love," as Gippius called it, when she still hoped for happiness.

> My heart is filled with the happiness of desire,
> With the happiness of possibility and expectation.
> But it trembles and fears
> That the expectation might be fulfilled.
> We don't dare to accept life fully,
> We cannot bear the weight of happiness,
> We want sounds, but fear harmony,
> We pine with the idle longing for limits,
> We love them eternally, eternally suffering—
> And we die, not attaining them . . .

A year later Gippius dedicated to him the poem "The Diamond" with the line mentioned at the beginning of this chapter about the brother who was Judas: "We thought we had a brother who was Judas." It was written after Filosofov, breaking with the Merezhkovskys, had left for Italy with Diaghilev.

The next poem is dated 1905 and is titled "Between." The end of 1905 was when Filosofov was trying to decide about the trip abroad and could not make up his mind.

> The branches darken against the moonlit sky
> Below, the rustling stream is barely heard
> While I swing in an airy net,
> Equally distant from heaven and earth.

Below is suffering, above—amusement.
Both pain and joy are hard for me.
The clouds are delicate, curly—like children.
The people are wretched and evil—like beasts.

I pity the people, I am ashamed of the children,
Here I won't be believed, there I won't be understood.
Below I am bitter, above I am pained.
And I am in a net—neither here nor there.

Those are all the poems she dedicated to Filosofov.
But Gippius continued to write about him and about her
feelings for him. It is not difficult to recognize such
poems. Here, for example, is one that could be a farewell
poem; it was written in September 1918:

Your sad star
Was briefly my joy:
It sparkled and fell
To the earth, a dark stone.

Your sad soul
Did not dare to love a smile,
And rushing from me,
It put on a black shroud.

But I joined my fate
To yours forever, in one hope:
Wherever you are, I am with you,
And I love you as before.

She remained true to him. Fidelity was a basic trait of her
nature. In one of her last poems she says to the doorkeeper guarding the entrance to Heaven:

Betrayal . . . No, old man, betrayal
Was not what I was guilty of.
I do not want to claim the credit,
But I have never betrayed love,
And I have never been unfaithful
To it or a woman or a friend.

I'm ready to be judged for the rest,
Let me be judged and come what may.

But the doorkeeper with a trembling hand opens the door before her and answers:

There'll be no judgment. You may pass!

XII

World War I divided them. I don't know whether Filosofov was a member of the Constitutional Democratic Party or if he only sympathized with it, but he published his articles in Milyukov's newspaper *Speech*, which was the organ of that party. The Merezhkovskys did not belong to any party. They thought the war was an unavoidable evil (they were against any kind of war on principle). There was no question for them of any justification for it, especially religious justification. In 1916 Gippius wrote:

No, I will not be reconciled.
My curses are the truth.
I'll not forgive, I will not fall
Into embrace of iron.
Like all who live I'll die, I'll kill,
Like all, destroy myself.
But I will never stain my soul
With justifying war.
In my last hour, in murk and fire,
Let my heart not forget
That war is never justified
And never shall it be.
And if it is the hand of God—
This gory, bloody road—
I shall arise and battle Him,
And wage a war on God.

That poem was, of course, not published then. No editor would have accepted it. It first appeared in the Berlin collection of Gippius' poetry, *A Diary*, which the publishing house The Word put out in 1922.

Filosofov regarded war differently. Not that he considered it a sacred cause, but he did support the patriotic spirit. War for him took precedence over everything. This was a source of constant clashes with the Merezhkovskys. They could see farther. For them the war was the beginning of a world wide disaster, something like the one described in *Secret of the West: Europe-Atlantis*. Gippius felt this particularly keenly. On the eve of the fateful year 1914, she wrote a poem which I have quoted more than once and which better than any other expresses her mental state at the time:

> A strange alarm weighs on my heart,
> Delirium of premonitions.
> I look ahead and the road is dark
> And perhaps there is no road.
>
> But I cannot touch with any words
> What is living in me—and in silence.
> I do not dare to feel it;
> It's like a dream. A dream within a dream.
>
> O, my incomprehensible alarm!
> It's more exhausting day by day.
> And I know that the grief on the threshold now,
> All that grief is not only for me.

When the disaster did strike (by the way, Gippius had predicted the Bolshevik victory as early as 1905. See "One Hour Before the Manifesto," her letter of October 17, 1905, to Filosofov, published in *La Renaissance*,[5]

5. *Vozrozhdenie* (*La Renaissance*), a Russian literary journal currently published in Paris, in which parts of this book were serialized in 1958.

number 64), relations between the Merezhkovskys and Filosofov had become so strained that they preferred not to speak to each other, because every conversation would lead to quarrels and arguments. Filosofov acted as if the Merezhkovskys were the cause of all the trouble, including the Bolshevik victory. He hardly ever left his room, staying in bed for days on end like a corpse, growing a beard and speaking to no one. He looked terrible. It was as if everything around him had turned to stone, including even the air. If it hadn't been for Merezhkovsky, who displayed exceptional energy and arranged their escape all by himself, he would have surely perished at the hands of the Bolsheviks.

The break with Filosofov occurred in Poland when the Merezhkovskys left for Paris and he remained in Warsaw together with Savinkov to continue the underground struggle against the Bolsheviks. Gippius took the break painfully. She sensed that Filosofov, no matter what happened to him or to Poland, would never return and that the break was now final. In her memoirs she was not being candid when she wrote that it was she, in part, who indirectly contributed to the break.

She came to hate Savinkov (in whose power Filosofov now was), having finally realized that he was above all else a stupid man. Nothing remained of her February Revolution attraction to Savinkov, when she had thought that only he and Kornilov could save Russia from destruction. And it was unbearable for her that Filosofov was in Savinkov's power.

After her death there was found among her papers a small notebook with a brown cover in the center of which was pencilled, "Give this to D. V. afterwards," that is, to Dmitry Vladimirovich Filosofov after her death. At the bottom left hand corner was the date: 1920. Under the inscription she wrote in ink, "There is no one to give it to. He is dead. He too. 1944."

Filosofov died on August 4, 1940, at the Polish resort of Otwock. The Merezhkovskys learned of his death in Biarritz, but not from Tèffi[6] as she wrote in her memoirs. In those memoirs published in *The New Russian Word*[7] on January 29, 1950, Tèffi, in order to prove that the Merezhkovskys were cold people, incapable of love, wrote about her encounter and conversation with them shortly after Filosofov's death. "Did they ever love anyone with a simple human love?" she asked, and answered: "I think not." She then described the conversation: "At one time they were very close to Filosofov. For a long time they were an inseparable trio. When the rumor reached Biarritz that Filosofov had died, I thought that the Merezhkovskys must be told. And that very day I ran into them on the street.

"'Have you heard the sad news about Filosofov?'

"'What is it? Did he die?' Merezhkovsky asked.

"'Yes.'

"'Do you know what of?' he asked, and without waiting for an answer he said, 'Come along now, Zina, or else we will again be late and they will run out of all the best dishes. We're having dinner in a restaurant today,' he explained to me. And that was all."

In the margin of that issue of *The New Russian Word* there was a note written by the woman who sent it to me and who was a great admirer of Tèffi: "Two disgusting,

6. Nadezhda Tèffi, the popular émigré short story writer and humorist.

7. *Novoe russkoe slovo*, the Russian-language daily, published in New York.

malicious libels" (i.e., of Merezhkovsky and Gippius).

What happened in fact was that the Merezhkovskys did not learn of Filosofov's death from Tèffi, but from Yakov Menshikov. In her daily calendar Gippius wrote on August 22, 1940: "Dmitry went out for a bit. He met Menshikov who told him that Dima had *died* August 4." And she added the last two lines of her "farewell poem":

> Wherever you are, I am with you,
> And I love you as before.

As for Tèffi, they simply did not want to discuss their loss with her. Merezhkovsky disliked her and thought her two-faced. Her account distorts their conversation.

In her diary *Gray and Red*, published in *The New Review*, Gippius wrote on September 2, 1940: "Since that day (August 22) when we met the ominous Menshikov and learned of Dima's death I have lived only with this one thought. I knew that he would die, that he was in pain and yearned for death. I even thought that he had already died, it was so hard to imagine that he could survive all that and survive his own self. Still and all, it is better not to know for sure. Here again is a confirmation that faith, any faith, my insignificant faith or a great faith, is always weaker than love. What can be simpler than to say like Solveig:

> God guard you, dear, where'er you be!
> . . . .
> If you're waiting above, I shall meet you there![8]

8. From Ibsen's *Peer Gynt*, quoted by Gippius in the Russian translation by Peter and Anna Hansen.

Yes, I will come. And if I don't come, I will never know I didn't. But the thought that I won't come and ever know . . ."

She survived Filosofov by five years. Her return trip began on the day of his death.

XIII

In the little notebook she had intended to leave for Filosofov there are sixty-four pages, fifty-two with notes written in pencil and twelve blank pages. The earliest entry is dated March 26, 1921, and the last one 1936. The day and the month are not indicated.

On March 26, 1921 Gippius wrote: "No ties. No aims. Just so. I don't understand: where does everything that passes through the soul disappear to? The unsaid. To yourself, without words. But *it was there*. That means it still exists. Or it was very 'verbal' and it didn't just flicker by; it endured, it could be remembered, but it wasn't told to anyone. Where did it go? Say I die. And where will it be? Where is it?

"And it is such that it was made to be passed on. But it will remain forever unknown to anyone. And there is so much of it."

She wrote further of separation, betrayal, and death. "In freely willed separation there is a concealed lie." (This is a line from her poem "Do not part while you live.") "It is so sweet to depart. I dreamt of my departure, it seems. I think of nothing. I carry within myself, within my entire being but one thing.

"In each little 'never again' are the extremely real eyes of death. The banality of that phrase is astonishing. It is astonishing because it has become banal *without becoming comprehensible.*

"But then, death is something that, more than anything else, is generally surrounded by a fence. When people say death, they mean its fence or, more often, they mean nothing.

"Basically, people cannot bear betrayal in others, the basic changes in their 'I.' People don't understand that they cannot bear it, yet they feel the most terrible indignation and rage over precisely that."

About Savinkov she wrote: "Perhaps Savinkov is nothing but mimicry. Has he disguised himself so thoroughly that he himself has come to believe his disguise? Riley* has definitely shelved him as the leader of the terrorist group.[9] He said: this is no *homme d'etat.* He said it was pointless to remain in Warsaw any longer and suggested that Savinkov cross the border illegally to join up with the still operating guerilla bands and that Antonov and Makhno[10] would accept him as a commander. Well, they won't.

"I feel very sorry for Savinkov. I have thought more about him. Or maybe I don't feel sorry. In him there is . . .

*Sidney Riley, Churchill's secretary, who spoke fluent Russian. He traveled several times, illegally, to the USSR. During one trip he was killed by the Bolsheviks.

9. "Sidney Riley" was actually a *nom de guerre* of Zygmunt Rosenblum, a Polish Jew who worked for the British intelligence.

10. A. S. Antonov was a Socialist Revolutionary leader, who organized a peasant rebellion against the Bolshevik dictatorship in the Tambov area in 1920–1922. Nestor Makhno, nicknamed "Batko" (i.e., "Daddy"), was an anarchist revolutionary who led the armed peasant resistance against the Bolshevik rule in the Ukraine which lasted for three years (1918–1921). Makhno's followers were known as "the Greens."

"All my indignation and all my outrage about the injustice of life has blended into a lump or hardened into a stone. I go about with that stone, I carry it in me and it makes me burst."

About Filosofov she wrote: "Dima, you basically have not changed. And in this lurks something terrible. A little bit of something terrible, but it is right there, in the persistence of your 'essence' which cannot change, but which is quite capable of changing its appearance."

Gippius meant that Filosofov had remained the same person he was before he had met Merezhkovsky and her. He had only seemed different. And that illusory quality horrified her. "You used to say that you had 'submitted' when you were with us (but to what?) and had lost your own personality and that you are responsible for your personality. And now?

"Savinkov might be a better mate for the external bent of your 'I' (it is hard to say) than Dmitry. But there is nothing particularly beautiful about that. It does your 'personality' no credit. (Because I'm saying this to myself, I don't have to dot the i's.)

"It's strange. I feel a certain relief because I don't constantly have to justify Dmitry to you, always feeling your critical and censuring gaze on him. I can allow him to be fallible in his own way, to be himself. I can protect him with my love without feeling shame.

"Your cruel constant judgment of him is your dark sin, Dima. But you will be forgiven for it because you had no choice. You didn't want to. But you could not stop. Just as you wanted to love me, but couldn't.

"Thinking of you, I do not ever judge you in any way. I'd rather pass judgment on myself. Especially myself. I do not have your excuses. I didn't do for you everything that I could have done. I knew how to love you as I wanted, i.e., as I could. But there is something that I didn't do with my love. There was much that I failed to do! Very much!"

She continued her entries in Wiesbaden where the Merezhkovskys spent the summer of 1921. The topics were the same: people, love, death.

"I feel no fear of my own death whatsoever. I am still a little afraid of the agony preceding death. Or perhaps I am very much afraid. But there is no bypassing it, now or later.

"And it is right *now* that I want peace. Sometimes I almost hallucinate: it is as if I were already looking back *from there*, speaking from there. All the sins of others seem so inconsequential, while my own are strangely clarified and grow heavy. That is the chief thing and the change is terribly vivid but inexpressible.

"At such times I don't even feel anger at the Bolsheviks (all anger becomes impossible). But it isn't forgiveness, nothing of the sort. Regarding the Bolsheviks, one begins to understand that they could have done nothing without God's permission. 'From here' I could still judge God, but 'from there' there is no thought of it, the idea doesn't enter my head, I don't know why."

The last entry for 1921 was on December 27: "No, I will never understand any kind of *betrayal*. No, 'betrayal' is too grand a word. I will never understand how something *was* and then is no longer.

"What is there not to understand? It is very simple. 'I do not grant my blessing.' Dima, you must remember those words as if they were your own. Perhaps that is why you are so angry, why your letter was so inordinately rude, so childishly unfair. That is why you feel such pity. Don't be ashamed to pity yourself.

"You will read this only if you survive me. Therefore you are sure to read it without fear or spite. But perhaps still without understanding, and I am prepared for that. Simply stop and look into your heart. After all, it was all right for you to leave *us* if we didn't suit you (or didn't please you), but not to leave the way you did. You couldn't leave what was once the chief thing for all of us. There is nowhere to escape and if you try, then there is no blessing for your deeds. I am not doing anything, although I didn't leave. I simply *collapsed* right where I stood.

"You write: it was the best time in my life (when you left) but I can see your clenched teeth. Where does your spite come from if you are satisfied with yourself and are happy?

"If one has nothing and has lost everything, one must not lose the truth. With just lies one cannot draw a single breath. And I will obtain the truth from God, even if I have to do it all alone."

Even if she did not obtain the Truth (with a capital T), she at least obtained the truth about Filosofov the following year, in 1922. She finally understood what had happened to him. The enemy had removed his mask and she recognized in him the same enemy she had been fighting all her life—the Devil. She did not utter his name, however. It was frightening that the person whose form he took was so close to her.

In the beginning of January 1922, Filosofov came to Paris on business. Before his arrival Gippius wrote down her impression of her last encounter with Savinkov who had taken her and Merezhkovsky out to dinner. "I did not hate Savinkov when I saw him last (the three of us had dinner together), *nor* did I pity him. I realized that I would never hate him or, for that matter, pity him. To tell the truth, I was bored. Not with what he was, but with what he had become. And not because of me, but because of him.

"Everything he was and everything he said was so unlike him that I did not see *him*. The one I did see seemed a bore. He has *moved on*, that is, what has happened to him is what happens most frequently these days and what is most comprehensible. He is a changeling. One more changeling.

"Could it be, Dima, that you too are already a changeling?" she asked Filosofov, knowing what had happened to him. "At least everything that comes from you in the realm of the phenomenal does not come from *you* and is not natural to you. It is as if it comes from some other person entirely.

"If that is so, then it is good that I no longer see you and it would perhaps be better that I not ever see you again. But no, not better, simply, it's all the same. I don't know if I'll reach that point, but I'd like to. To achieve the stage of full knowledge that you have not perished, but that you live within me, in my (aching) heart, the only real you, you yourself.

"'Where was I, I myself?' Peer Gynt asked, alarmed, at a fateful moment. And for him, as for you, that place exists. Have no fear.

"But when I think in this manner, I do not feel like letting you read these words, even after my death. It seems unnecessary. To give them to you is to give them to another, for in the realm of the phenomenal you are not him, and it is another who will be reading these words. The categories are confused and we must first separate them completely so that later they may blend. I need great strength in order to preserve you faithfully. To preserve you in the pure state, distinct and whole, not darkened by anything that is mine, not by the slightest shadow."

XIV

Filosofov arrived in Paris on January 3, 1922. The Merezhkovskys had prepared a room for him in their home. But he stayed at the Hôtel d'Auteuil on the rue d'Auteuil. On the night of January 4 Gippius wrote: "Well, and here is dearest Dima. Yesterday 'he' arrived in Paris. He sent a *petit bleu* to V. [Zlobin—S. K.] asking to come by the hotel to see him. *You*, of course, would have come immediately. It would be ridiculous to imagine that he is you. Have I separated you completely, that is, even physically, from the changeling? It seems I have not entirely succeeded, but I am working on it and I will get there.

"You and I understand, don't we, why 'he' cannot be indifferent, why he is spiteful for no apparent reason, why he speaks with such malicious spite, trying to be disdainful, about the 'unshakable Merezhkovskys' and all the rest? That is his impotence, and besides, he is constantly giving himself away, betraying that he isn't you, my radiant one, my own, my poor sweet thing. He doesn't know that you are alive, although he has driven you out of yourself. But he vaguely suspects something and he is afraid."

Those last lines were apparently written after Filosofov's visit. He came on Janaury 9, that is, a week after his arrival. The night before he came, Gippius had a dream. "The night before January 9 I had such a dreadful dream," she wrote. "Dima was dying in the next room (it was an unfamiliar apartment), and for some reason I couldn't go in. I paced from corner to corner. Then he died and a maid (was it a hotel?) closed his eyes. And I could only peek in through the door. I saw only his back on the bed. I woke up feeling like a wreck physically. I fell asleep again and again the same thing. It was a continuation. That was the day you came, Dima (you or he). I did all I could to help him seem to be you. For that one needs only to speak of nothing."

It was as if Filosofov had stepped out of the nightmare that tormented her. But most frightening of all, the nightmare did not go away once she was awake. On the contrary, reality turned into a nightmare. The double, the changeling was getting the upper hand.

The transformation of Filosofov had political consequences as well. Gippius was aware of it: "The Dima who followed and still follows Savinkov step by step, from intervention to uprising, to the Greens, to workers' councils without the Commune, then to His Majesty the Russian peasant, and then to Heaven knows what else, does not notice that it will bring him to Lenin without the Cheka,[11] that is, to absurdity. I will not speak with him about it for my sake and for his. He will try to justify it all by politics and I do not want to subject my ailing heart to more useless pain. There is no need."

11. *Cheka* is an acronym of "Extraordinary Commission," Lenin's political police that carried out the post-revolutionary terror.

She understood even Savinkov, as reflected through Filosofov, for what he was, not for what he seemed. In 1923, a year after her last encounter with him, she wrote: "Sometimes it seems to me that there hasn't been any Savinkov for a long time and you are in the hands of an evil mirage, a specter. I'm not afraid to say it, a plaything of the Devil, yes! Yes! After all, the Devil has no body and those are the kinds of playthings he has. That *puppet* Savinkov is not a frightening puppet. Only to those who don't know what he is. True, nature does not like, cannot stand his kind, for he is *emptiness*. I myself do not know when I came to such an irrevocable formula (and with that meaning)—emptiness. But the meaning is that Savinkov is worse than any Bolshevik, than Trotsky, for example. That is, he is beyond the pale of anything human or divine.

"Now that I have said it, I am frightened. How dare I speak like that? Perhaps it is personal, because of you, Dima, when I see that he drove you out of yourself.

"I am myself becoming blurred. I speak and I don't dare speak, I know and I do not want to know, I believe that I know nothing. Let God see and judge Savinkov. I cannot and dare not. I am silent. I am silent."

Then suddenly she became outraged. She tried to be humble, but nothing came of it. "At times I am seized by rebellion. And what rebellion!" she admitted in December 1923. "I am not afraid, not of you, Dima, nor for you. I don't care what low words I use as I curse, and being benign is for me the same as being unctuous. And it is not words I need, but some kind of knife with which I wouldn't hesitate to *cut* you away from Savinkov, whatever it might cost. You would recover or die and I don't care about Savinkov—who cares about an empty spot like him!"

But she was not sure a "knife" would help. "I know that even then you would not recover *completely*. You would never have the strength to return to the past (the truth). Not even then. But that is not essential, that is, it is essential, but it would not be a consideration for me. If only you would recover a little. That is, I know that even after you were cut away from Savinkov you would never forgive me *for being right*. And that's just why, and not because I was so guilty (for which I can never forgive myself). But almost no one can forgive another person for being right. What pain. What pain."

Finally we come to 1924, the year of Savinkov's betrayal, his going over to the Bolsheviks. Gippius wrote in November: "Can it be? Can it really have happened? Dima, God decided as I had not expected. How happy I am these days. I saw *you* recovered or on your way to recovery. After these weeks of this unbelievable nightmare (on your account), what an unexpected joy! This notebook has lost its purpose. It is now a souvenir, just for myself. So I can say 'Didn't I tell you?' But it isn't at all necessary.

"Instead of Savinkov, an empty vile spot has been revealed and I think it was a miracle for your sake that that emptiness was revealed so that you could see it. Thank God for you; I knew you would not perish 'there', but what great fortune that this was given to us here. And even if your wound aches and you conceal your pain by an act of will—don't worry, it's nothing. Everything will be, that is, everything already is, for *you* are again you."

Six months passed. In May 1925 word was received from Moscow of Savinkov's "suicide." It was claimed that he had "thrown himself" from the window of his prison. "That made no impression on me," Gippius wrote. "Whether he killed himself or whatever else might have happened—isn't it all the same? After all, he's been dead for years. Did he really ever exist? Dima, you still will not forgive me (or you won't forget) that *I was right*."

Eleven years passed. What she lived through in that time is expressed by Gippius in the single line which ends her manuscript: "Yes, that happened *too late* (for D.)."

In 1943, two years before her death, she dedicated her last poem to Filosofov:

> There was a time when I was loved
> By his own Psyche, by his Love.
> He did not credit what he was told
> By Holy Spirit, not flesh and blood.
> He thought his Psyche was his deception,
> That flesh and blood were his only truth.
> He followed them instead of Psyche,
> He hoped to find his Love through them.
> But all he did was lose his Psyche.
> And what once was, will never be.
> Psyche departed and with her
>   I lost his love.

That was the *only* poem in which Gippius wrote of herself in the feminine gender.[12] And that, of course, was not by chance.

---

12. Zlobin is mistaken, for there exist several other poems by Gippius in which she speaks of herself in the feminine gender.

FIVE

Gippius and the Devil

Gippius first mentioned the Devil in the poem "Griselda," written in 1895. Griselda, in a castle awaiting the return of her husband from war, suffered "unheard of misfortunes." The "Lord of Evil" himself tried to tempt her.

> Griselda is victorious,
> And Satan lost his power.
> The Evil One is bowing
> To Virtue's fairest flower.
> Griselda is triumphant,
> Her soul is shining bright.
> But still, how strong the spirit
> Of lies and darkest night.

And Gippius exclaims:

> O, tell me, Wisest Tempter,
> Dark Spirit—could you be
> The misconstrued Preceptor
> Who teaches us Beauty?

But in 1895 she was not the only one to exclaim like that. Russian poets of the Silver Age were tied to the French Symbolists by more than their name. The question of the Devil and the problem of evil had been raised already by Baudelaire and Verlaine. Their influence on the Russian Symbolists in this area is undeniable. The seed fell on fertile soil.

The following quatrain deserves special attention:

> Griselda is triumphant,
> Her soul is shining bright.
> But still, how strong the spirit
> Of lies and darkest night.

Here, in the last two lines, we see the change from contemplation to action, still timid, not fully realized, but already fatally irrepressible. But then, the poison worked slowly. Seven years were to pass before she expressed with her usual, utmost clarity her feelings about the Devil in a poem called "God's Creature." In the interval, in 1901—that is, a year earlier—she wrote some lines not understandable to the uninitiated about a monster which kept calling her somewhere and promising her salvation:

> My solitude is infinite and limitless,
> But it's so stifling and so narrow;
> And an affectionate monster has crawled up to me,
> It looks into my eyes and thinks—I don't know what.

It took her a long time to discover what it was thinking. But here is what she herself thought of the monster:

> I offer prayers for the Devil,
> O, Lord! He is your creature.
> I love the Devil, for I see
> My suffering within him.
>
> In torment and in struggle
> He weaves his nets with care.
> And I cannot help but pity
> The one who suffers as I do.
>
> When our flesh shall rise again
> For retribution at Thy judgment,
> Forgive him then, O Lord, his sins,
> His madness for his pain.

She shares the Devil's suffering with him fraternally—it is the result of their joint madness. We will find out later just what that madness was. Let us now speak of her three encounters with the Devil. The first one is described in the poem "Into a Line," dated 1905. I quote it in its entirety:

> He came to me—I don't know who he is.
> He encircled me within a ring.
> He said that I don't know who he is,
> But he hid his face behind a cape.
>
> I begged him to tarry longer,
> To step back, not touch me, and to wait.
> If he only could but tarry longer
> And not enclose me within that ring.
>
> The Dark One was amazed: "What can I do?"
> Quietly he laughed under his cloak.
> "Your own sin encircles you. What can I do?
> Your own sin enclosed you in that ring."
>
> As he left he also said: "You're wretched!"
> As he left he sank into a void.
> "Break the ring around you. Don't be wretched!"
> Break and stretch it out into a line."
>
> So he left, but he will yet return.
> So he left and never showed his face.
> What am I to do if he returns?
> There's no way that I can break the ring.

What is immediately striking here is that the Devil comes to her not as a tempter, for her fall took place before his arrival, but merely to draft something like an official record. Speaking modern Russian, what he does is "establish the facts." Furthermore, it should also be noted that he behaves not in the least diabolically. He tries to wound her pride, obviously in order to help her "break the ring," i.e., to escape from an unpleasant predicament for which she is herself responsible. Who he really is, is not known. However, there is every reason to assume that hiding under that cape is an angel, not the Devil.

The second encounter took place thirteen years later in September, 1918, in St. Petersburg (please note the date). She described it in the poem "The Hour of Victory." The title is highly promising.

> Again he came, he looks at me with scorn
> (I don't know who he is, just Someone in a cape)
> And he laughs, "Oh, this is getting tiresome,
> The circumstances cry to end it all.
> I'm tired of watching you in wretched battle,
> The minutes of my time have now been numbered.
> Your circles are still whole, not one is broken,
> Nor have you stretched them out into a line.
> Has not your soul yet had its fill of dreams?
> I have no use for dreams that last too long.
> I'll forge you rings of iron and of steel
> And permanently solder you inside them."
> He took his gloves off with a vicious smile
> And grasped the ends of my enclosing ring.
> But with his own black glove I struck
> The alien creature right across the face.
> No! Only blood alone will ever solder
> Or else unsolder and break up my ring.
> His cape fell off, blown by a sudden gust,
> And I could see a corpse-like face.
> I looked into his so familiar eyes,
> I looked and then he sank into a void.
> And it was then that my victorious ring
> Stretched out into a flaming line.

And so the Devil returned. Gippius's premonition did not deceive her. But it was no longer a "decadent" devil in a romantic cape, but a devil of 1918 in a stylish caped overcoat, with gloves (black ones, what else?), an *agent provocateur* of the Cheka. She defeated him with the magical word "blood" (yet why should he fear blood? Wasn't he wearing gloves because his hands were covered with it?). Like his predecessor he also "sank into a void." But Gippius's victory was only on paper. The Devil "sank into a void" solely out of respect for her literary status. Otherwise there would have been no need for him to appear for the third time.

The third encounter took place after she had emigrated. The date is not indicated (it can be dated approximately between 1925 and 1930). Gippius described this encounter with her usual mastery in the poem "Indifference":

> Now he's different when he comes.
> He assumes a slave-like guise.
> And bows down so very humbly,
> Sits down quietly in the corner,
> At a distance from me, on the floor,
> Snickering insincerely.
>
> He whispers: "I dropped by, my love,
> Just like that, just to have a look.
> I won't bother you—I wouldn't dare.
> I'll sit for a while in my corner.
> If you're tired, I shall amuse you,
> I can do a whole lot of tricks.
>
> Want to look into your fellow men?
> You'll just die, it's so screamingly funny!
> Name me anyone you like,
> Point out anyone to me,

And I'll change you into him
Just like that, on my word of honor,

For an instant, but not forever,
So you'll stand in his shoes for a while.
If you're in them for only a moment,
You will know what is truth, what is lies.
You will see through him—through and through.
Once you do, you won't soon forget.

What's the matter with you? Chat with me.
It's no fun? Now wait just a minute,
I know some other tricks too."
Thus he whispered and babbled in his corner,
Wretched, puny, he sat on the floor,
Wringing his thin little hands.

And a secret fear consumed him:
Of my answer. He waited and withered,
Promising me he'd be good.
But this time I did not raise my eyes
From my work to look at him.
I stayed silent and was indifferent.

Go away or stay here with me;
Go ahead and wiggle, but my calm
Won't be ruined by the likes of you.
And he melted before my eyes,
Before my eyes he dissolved into dust,
Because I was indifferent.

I offer my apologies for such a long quotation. It will
be the last long one. Because of it we can now congratu-
late the Devil. Now, for the first time, he is behaving as
a devil should. He is actually a tempter, even though he
appeared in the form of a "trembling creature." In spite
of his degraded, wretched state he does not give up until
the last moment. She pretended she didn't notice him, as

if he weren't there, and because of her scornful indifference he melts and dissolves into dust.

But Gippius's indifference was a sham. Actually it was
she and not the Devil who was consumed by a secret fear
and she tried to hide it from him with all the means at
her disposal. But the Devil was also pretending. He only
pretended to tempt her because, as her poetry testifies,
she had long since yielded to the temptation of looking
into the souls of her fellow men in order to see the insignificance of the people around her (especially of those
closest to her). Here is one of the most typical of these
poems, "Admonition":

> Be silent. Be silent. Don't talk to people,
> Don't lift the veil from your heart.
> All the people on earth—please understand!—
> Are not worth one single word.
>
> Don't cry. Don't cry. Blessed is he
> Who chose to hide his pain from people.
> This world's not worth a single tear,
> Your tear or that of anyone.
>
> Hold back, feel ashamed to show your suffering,
> Withdraw and pass on calmly.
> The earth, the people don't deserve
> Your words, your tears, your sighs. Nothing.

Here is another, no less convincing:

> It seemed I would never again
> Disturb the silence of my soul,
> But a star flared up in the window,
> And again I pity my soul.
> Everything died long ago in my soul.
> Hatred and anger burned out.
> O, my poor soul, just one thing
> Is preserved in it: scornful contempt.

What, after all, could the Devil want from her and why was she so mortally afraid? After describing her "Hour of Victory" so brilliantly, she came to understand (it was so obvious that, given her mind, she could not help understanding it) that, apart from her poetic casuistry which concealed, in essence, a fairly primitive rationalism, she had no weapon against the Devil. From the point of view of religious consciousness, this was a total failure, a failure which was, it is true, somewhat unexpected, considering the heights she had seemingly attained in that area. But if ever her genius revealed itself in its full power, it was precisely at the moment when she created a defense against the Devil, a weapon which under certain conditions could save her from destruction.

She knew by premonition that she was sure to encounter the Devil again. She knew that on that last occasion he would range against her all the forces of Hell and she saw to it that in that terrible hour she would not have to face him empty-handed. One of the prerequisites for victory was secrecy: no one was supposed to know anything about it. She tried to prevent even God from "getting a glimpse and overhearing." Otherwise her weapon would lose its potency.

However, the Devil managed to get an inkling of something or other (perhaps it reached him through God, after all). He became uneasy. He had to find out at any cost what was going on, so he assumed a "slave-like guise" and appeared to Gippius for the third time. That was the real reason for his visit. We know that his failure was complete. Gippius did not utter a word and he had to withdraw empty-handed.

We will learn later what weapon Gippius had at her disposal from that time on and what its salutary powers were. Let us return for the moment to the problem of the Devil as "God's Creature." Gippius was not only not in conflict with this "second" Devil, but on the contrary she shared with him fraternally his suffering, the result of their joint madness. In order to avoid confusion, though, we must always remember that no matter what guise the Devil might assume, no matter what feelings he might arouse, he is still the same Devil, the same destroyer of men that he always has been and always will be. But the duality of her religious consciousness was the greatest danger that Gippius faced. The danger was that her metaphysical victory over the Devil would lose its inner meaning and become as if it had never happened. And her genuine weapon against the Devil, the result of her victory, would cancel itself out, would be turned into something highly unattractive from the point of view of human morality, for how can one raise a hand against "our poor suffering brother?" This, of course, would suit the Devil just fine.

What is meant, however, by the "madness" of the Devil, the madness which Gippius so imprudently shares with him? It is not so easy to answer that question and it is possible that my somewhat amateurish approach to such an important topic may seem superficial to the enlightened reader. I ask the reader's forbearance in advance. What the Devil wants, has always wanted, both before and after his fall (it was the cause of his fall), is to enjoy eternal bliss alone with God. Outside of that, he wants nothing else to exist. "Les amoureux sont seuls au monde"—for those in love the world does not exist. But God is a trinity and by negating the world, the Devil negates the trinity of the Deity, negates His most secret essence, outside of which there is nothing, that is, nothing is possible and love is most impossible of all. It was not by accident that in 1922 Gippius wrote in her diary: "All suffering comes from love. From all kinds of love, conscious and unconscious, because all love (life) is loss."

For the modern-day Devil, man, mankind, and world history are but a barrier between himself and God. He tries to destroy that barrier and is tireless in his destructiveness. But the more he tries to draw near God, the farther God is from him. The contradiction is irreconcilable and that irreconcilability is the cause of the Devil's suffering and madness. He exists in a state akin to eternal falling. Many of the poems by Gippius that seem to us obscure become clear in light of this. One need not search far for an example. Here is the poem "All the Same":

> From this exhausting weakness
>   Nowhere to go! Nowhere to go!
> Which flows around my heart
>   Like water! Like water!
>
> Was it really written—(and by whom?)—
>   In the heavens,
> That two demons, hope and fear,
>   Should eat into my soul?
>
> I won't be saved, I have been struggling
>   For so long! For so long!
> I'm sure to fall, let me reach the bottom,
>   But where's the bottom?

She felt that the pit was bottomless. But she never understood until the very last moment that the name of the pit was madness, the same madness that she shared with the Devil. At the very beginning of the 1890s, when Merezhkovsky was still elaborating the idea of duality—"heaven above, heaven below"—in his novels *Julian the Apostate* and *Leonardo da Vinci*, she was absorbed in working out one idea which became for her a kind of *idée fixe*, as she put it in her book on Merezhkovsky. That idea was the "trinitarian structure of the world." She was undoubtedly sincere in her enthusiasm. But while she was working out her *idée fixe* in terms of its application to daily life, she was again confronted with the problem of evil, which, if left unsolved, would render her idea an abstract scheme, a stillborn infant (if there was anything that the Devil disliked, it was the trinitarian structure of the world). And here, despite their novel sound, one senses a strange emptiness behind her words, an emptiness that could be explained only by the absence of personal experience.

This was unexpected and justifiably astonishing. She seemed to be and indeed was an extremely balanced person. But her spiritual equilibrium was not really an equilibrium, but only the impossibility of inner conflict. Her soul was peculiarly constructed: good and evil alternated in it but did not clash. When an angel made an entrance, the Devil would vanish and vice versa. More and more it began to seem to her that it was one and the same person, one who could change costumes in the wings with the agility of a Fregoli.[1] But there was great confusion in her emotions.

These changes were instantaneous. From their endless flickering and swaying her head began to spin and her constant feeling of nausea grew worse. "I'm as nauseated as if I were in hell," she would say later. She became physically weakened.

1. Leopold Fregoli, 1867–1936, a famous quick-change artist, mime, and illusionist.

> All my "I" swings like a pendulum,
>   And its sweep is very wide.
> It sways, slides, alternates:
>   Now it's hope, now it's fear.
>
> From knowing, from not knowing, from flickering
>   My flesh is dying.
> Can you condemn it, O Lord!,
>   This painful, insane swaying?
>
> End it and stop the rippling torment.
>   Halt it! Halt it!
> Only not at the terror of falling,
>   But at love's upward swing.

But her prayer was not heard. The pendulum continued to sway. Only its sweep was gradually growing shorter. In 1934, fifteen years after she had secured her victory over the Devil, she wrote the following four lines in the poem "November 8" (her birthday):

> It smells of roses and inevitability.
> Who will help and how can they help?
> Eternal changes, eternal contiguities,
> Summer and fall, day and night.

In those simple, sparse lines, which are like tearful children's faces to which no one pays any attention, lies the whole tragedy of her soul. And the pendulum still swings. Now it is hope:

> I believe in the happiness of liberation,

now it is fear:

> It's frightening because I do not live, I sleep.
> And everything splits into two, into four.

In the 1930s, in connection with Merezhkovsky's book *The Unknown Jesus*, she dedicated to him an eight-line poem in which she spoke out against excessive philosophizing about Christ's resurrection, the kind of philosophizing to which Merezhkovsky was always somewhat inclined:

> Do not strive for replies as we travel,
> Do not touch the light linen web,
> Do not look for footprints in the dust—
> Do not search for impossible words.
>
> See how blissful the children are,
> Let us also be simple in heart.
> There are no other words in the world
> Save the ultimate words of St. Thomas.

"My Lord and my God!" But hardly had she uttered those words when something terrible happened. For one instant a demon entered her and she wheezed in a voice not her own:

> When I was resurrected from the dead,
> One thing amazed me:
> That resurrection from the dead
> And all that had ever been
> Was just as it ought to be.
> I should have guessed it before!
> And disappointment gnawed at me,
> That I hadn't guessed in time.

In 1918, in the dead St. Petersburg over which "sin was spread," when she tearfully repeated "My heart be resurrected! Be resurrected!" a voice familiar to her since childhood whispered: "Resurrection is not for everyone." And now she thought she had already been resurrected. Fine! Therefore, to mark the day of her premature resurrection there was a gift for her: a red Easter egg. She actually wrote and signed her name to the following lines:

Don't give in to any hope
And don't believe your regrets for the past.
Don't say it was better before.
For our terrible Now was hidden

In our Before as in a serpent's egg.
Not all of the shell is yet broken,
There are a few cracks. Have a look:
The serpent merely showed its head,
And there are many baby serpents in the egg.

Watch coldly, without disgust:
They crawl in a slippery line,
They crawl and follow after the first serpent,
Winding tightly into coil after coil.

Oh yes! That which we call the earth—
Isn't the whole of it a serpent's egg?

To prove that Gippius was not herself when she wrote that poem, I will quote the first and last stanzas of her poem "God's Own," written in November 1916:

Beloved, faithful, Betrothed for all time,
My purest almond tree blossom,
Awakened to love by God's breath,
My joy—my Earth!

. . . .

I love the whole of you, my Only One,
The whole of you is mine!
Together we'll be resurrected beyond a mysterious bound-
ary,
Together—both you and I.

However, there is nothing new about this self-contradiction. It has always been there to a lesser or greater extent and it was reflected in her poetry perhaps not in such a categorical form, but every bit as expressively. For example, here is the beginning of her poem "The Earth," written in 1908:

> And the deserted orb in empty desert,
> Like meditation of the Devil,
> Suspended always, still hangs there . . .
> Madness! Madness!

At that time she still realized that to see the world as she sometimes depicted it was madness. Now, however, when she was actually sinking to the bottom, she did not realize her madness, or, at any rate, she did not call it by its name. Here is perhaps the most terrifying of all her poems:

> The waves of otherworldly nausea foam up,
> Break into spray and scatter in black mist,
> And into darkness, into outermost darkness,
> As they return to subterranean ocean.
>
> We call it pain here, sorrowful and heartfelt,
> But it's not pain, for pain is something else.
> For subterranean and endless nausea
> There are no earthly words, for words are not enough.
>
> A living net of hopes is cast beneath us,
> Delivering us from every kind of pain—
> Hope for a new encounter, friendship, or oblivion
> Or, finally, the hope that we shall die.
>
> Be grateful, Dante, that you did not learn all
> About the dwelling of the dead, through your friend's
>   care,
> That your companion drew you from the circle,

The ultimate one, and you did not see it.
And even if you hadn't died of terror,
You still would not have told us what you saw.

It would appear that Gippius had looked deeper into hell than Dante. But she remained silent about what was revealed to her in the last circle. That is not such a great secret, though, because the Devil is a logician and a mathematician and his goal is always the same. There, at the bottom of hell, in the last circle, she could see with her own eyes that *God was the Devil*. Her madness was the Devil's logic carried to its ultimate conclusion.

After her death a poem was found among her papers where the speaker is apparently the Devil who has finally dropped all pretense to courteous behavior and who shows himself for the boor he is. He is apparently sitting across the table from her in the guise of her closest friend and he is thinking about something in silence. But she can guess his thoughts (which isn't hard since he is inside her). I will cite the last stanza of this truly Smerdyakovian[2] poem:

I watch those senile lips that drool.
In stony silence I am lost.
Think what you want to, you old fool,
But I forgot the Holy Ghost.

How was she saved? Several days before November 8, 1918—her birthday (I remind you, she was born on the

2. Derived from the name of Smerdyakov, a degenerate character in Dostoevsky's *The Brothers Karamazov*. In the context of the poem "Not by Bread Alone" (1944) Gippius ascribed these thoughts to Vladimir Zlobin, not the Devil.

day of Archangel Michael and all the heavenly hosts)—
when she was in Bolshevik-occupied St. Petersburg, she
wrote a poem called "Days":

> All days are fractured as though by crime,
> The passage of hoary time grows rusty,
> My body's fettered with rigidity,
> My heart oppressed and my blood cold as ice.
>
> But there comes lightning: everything can change
> In a prophetic dream or wide awake.
> The sword of the Archangel touches me
> With burning flame and I'm alive again!

That flame was an eight-line poem titled "8" which
she wrote on November 8 of that same year, on her
birthday. But she did not write down the last two lines
of the second stanza, each line containing four words.
Instead she used dashes. Here is that poem as she wrote it
in her rough draft notebook, her "verse laboratory," and
copied it down in her "Bryusov notebook" which Valery
Bryusov had given to her as a present:

8

> Eight words burn in my heart,
> But I will never dare to say them.
> There is a line which no one ever mentions
> Because this line cannot be crossed.
> And all the same, no one will understand
> That through these words there courses human blood:
> "_____ _____ _____ _____
>
> _____ _____ _____ _____"

She showed these six lines to a close friend who had come
to wish her a happy birthday and she asked him: "Can
you guess?" That was a test. She was afraid that it would
be possible to reconstruct the last two lines because in

Russian "love" is frequently rhymed with "blood." But the person she asked understood neither the lines nor the poem, and she was reassured.

Twenty-seven years passed; she died and carried her secret to the grave. It was in order to extort that secret from her that the Devil had appeared to her for the third time. And if he met with no success, it was only because the "magic words" were never, not even once, uttered aloud by anyone, not even by herself. But perhaps the poem "There are Words" was written in June 1918 as a kind of premonition of those "magic words."

> Everyone has his special magic words,
> And on the surface they mean nothing,
> But when they are recalled, they flash and slip right by
> And yet our heart begins to laugh and cry.
>
> I don't like to repeat them, for I guard
> Them from myself, forgetting them on purpose.
> But I will meet them on the other shore,
> For they are written on the gates of Heaven.

We will never know those words. Their exact meaning is irrevocably lost to us. But if we possess an ounce of imagination and try to imagine her life at the end of 1918 in Bolshevik St. Petersburg, try to understand her spiritual condition at the time, and the problem that tormented her most of all just then, and if we add to all that some audacity, to say nothing of personal intuition, then these are approximately the eight words she did not write down:

8

> Eight words burn in my heart,
> But I will never dare to say them.
> There is a line which no one ever mentions

Because this line cannot be crossed.
And all the same, no one will understand
That through these words there courses human blood:
"But   God   calls   freedom
What   we   call   love."

But what is the power of these seemingly simple, ordinary words? It resides in the following: "To him that
overcometh will I give to eat of the hidden manna, and
will give him a white stone, and in the stone a new name
written, which no man knoweth saving he that receiveth
it" (Revelations 2:17). That new name is FREEDOM,
the new name of love and the ultimate revelation of the
Divine Triunity. This name is given to "him that overcometh" together with "hidden manna"—the source of
indestructible spiritual power—and it enables him who
partakes of the manna to achieve communion with divine
nature.

But why eight words? It was more important to her in
that poem than anywhere else to emphasize that she was
born on the day the Archangel Michael was victorious
over the Devil and that she was under his protection. But
that reason was not the chief one.

The chief reason is this. The number of the cross is
four; the eight words burning in her heart were like a
burning cross becoming two in the quivering flames,
symbolizing in essence the double sacrifice—of God for
the sake of the world and of the world for the coming of
the Holy Ghost: "Thy Kingdom come."

And when the storm of death descended upon her
from the depths of eternity, when the forces of hell come
crashing down upon her and for the first time she found
herself face to face with the enemy without his mask,
then even the Archangel Michael with his hosts, who

were aiding her in her battle, could not have saved her if at that moment she had not held in her hands an invincible weapon: a Cross of Flame.

SIX

One Hour Before
the Manifesto

Zinaida Gippius was fiercely anti-Bolshevik. Her attitude toward the Social Democratic Party was fully defined as early as 1905, as can be seen from her letter of December 7, 1905, to Dmitry Filosofov. In the top right hand corner of the first page there is the note: "Written one hour before the Manifesto."[1] Quite apart from the political significance of that document, one cannot deny that Gippius was perceptive or that she strove for an objective evaluation of the events then taking place in Russia and, in particular, of the activities of the Social Democratic Party, its program and its methods of implementing that program.

The significance that Gippius ascribed to the Social Democrats, now called Bolsheviks,[2] and her absolute certainty of their ultimate victory might have seemed, and to many people did in fact seem, exaggerated in 1905. Today those realized prophecies seem like a pale

1. The so-called October Manifesto of 1905, issued by Nicholas II as the result of the revolutionary events of that year, guaranteed civil liberties and established a parliament (Duma). This document in effect changed Russia from an autocratic empire to a constitutional monarchy. The unwillingness of the government of Nicholas II to abide by the provisions of the October Manifesto and its sabotage of their implementation led to further revolutionary ferment that culminated in the February and October Revolutions.

2. Throughout this chapter Zlobin confuses the Bolsheviks, who in 1905 were one of the factions of the Social Democratic party, with the whole of that party.

outline compared to what we Russians have lived through and what awaits us and our descendants in the future. Dostoevsky's "demonology" (in *The Possessed*), which analyzed the true nature of Bolshevism with astonishing accuracy and even predicted the exact time of the coup (right after the Feast of the Protection of the Virgin), offers a clearer and much more frightening picture. All that, however, is true only as long as we remain within the framework of a particular text. Gippius herself expressed her reservations at the beginning of her letter: "I write all this," she added in parentheses, "without any reasoning, without metaphysics, not at all in my usual way. From a different angle."

No, it wasn't that Gippius did not have enough imagination or that she failed to grasp the atmosphere of the Bolshevik October Revolution. On the contrary, few people sensed the deadly nature of the storm threatening the world as Gippius sensed it and few observed its approach with such great alarm. Most of her writings, especially her poetry, are filled with this prophetic alarm. As the fateful year 1914 approached, she wrote:

> A strange alarm weighs on my heart,
> Delirium of premonitions.
> I look ahead and the road is dark
> And perhaps there is no road.
>
> But I cannot touch with any words
> What is living in me—and in silence.
> I do not dare to feel it:
> It's like a dream. A dream within a dream.
>
> O, my incomprehensible alarm!
> It's more exhausting day by day.
> And I know that the grief on the threshold now,
> All that grief is not only for me.

But the misfortune was that, while she sensed the impending catastrophe with her entire being (the poem is called "On the Threshold"), she could not find a name for it, did not connect it with any mundane reality, did not realize that the nightmare of perdition that kept suffocating her all her life and before whose vision she grew mute with terror was the inevitable consequence of the inevitable victory of the Bolsheviks, accomplishing their dark ends in full view of everyone.

That is why in her letter to Filosofov she, typically, did not foresee the interim February Revolution, having considered the Bolsheviks the only possible victors and having seen nothing ominous in their eventual victory. In that disjunction between feeling and consciousness, in the fact that her will was constantly divided against itself, in the occasional total paralysis of that will was the tragedy not only of Gippius, but also of many of her contemporaries.

As for the document itself, her letter to Filosofov, it is dated Monday, October 17, 1905. In the upper left hand corner there is a quotation from the Gospels: "By their works shall ye know them." Next to it is a note in pencil: "Written one hour before the Manifesto." At the beginning of this chapter I had wanted to place as an epigraph the last four lines of Merezhkovsky's poem "Cassandra":

> You knew the path to secret lines,
> And in the daylight you saw night.
> But the revenge of fates on prophets
> Is to know all, yet lack the might.

The Manifesto of October 17, 1905, was an obstacle in the path of the Bolsheviks, as Loris-Melikov's project for a constitution would have been if Alexander II had lived to sign it.[3] But he was killed on March 1, 1881. Alexander III, therefore, found the project premature and refused to sign it, thereby playing into the hands of the revolutionaries. Yet the proposed reforms were quite modest. It was not a question of introducing into Russia a parliamentary system along English lines, but only of creating an advisory body made up of elected representatives from various social strata. For the same reasons P. A. Stolypin was assassinated by the very same revolutionaries during the reign of Nicholas II. His land reforms were also among the obstacles in the path of the Revolution.[4]

But let us return to Gippius's letter. "That internal terror," she continued with considerable expertise, "will distract the peasants from any attempts at uprisings against the Provisional Government, which is sure to have the power to suppress them by force. After all, it will have to hold on to power, which it will be able to do only by force." But here Gippius seems to awake from her hypnotic trance, and her prophetic vision grows dim. Here is what she wrote about the calling of a constituent assembly (which she says "the Bolsheviks do not want") and about its function: "At last there will be a general

3. Count Mikhail Loris-Melikov had drafted proposals for extending the liberalizing reforms of Alexander II and establishing a more representative form of government in Russia. The assassination of Alexander II by revolutionary terrorists in 1881 prevented the implementation of the Loris-Melikov project.

4. Stolypin's land reforms of 1906 and 1911 were aimed at strengthening the individual peasant land holdings. Zlobin's point is that Russian revolutionaries systematically opposed all measures that would lead to greater political freedom or economic equality under the old regime, seeing that kind of improvement as inimical to their cause.

constituent assembly which can *peacefully* [the italics are hers] work out the general communist statutes. I forgot to say that they [the Bolsheviks] are not afraid of the bourgeoisie and again they are ever so right."

But unfortunately we know that the Constituent Assembly elected under the Bolsheviks was a victory for the Socialist Revolutionaries, who had an absolute majority in that first Russian parliament. We also know the Assembly was dispersed by the Bolsheviks and we know the role that the sailor Zheleznyak[5] played in that affair. Incidentally, Alexander Kerensky tells in his recent memoirs published in *The New Review* how he was present at that Assembly, more or less in disguise.[6]

But the physical bonds with Russia, the bonds of the flesh, the bonds to one's mother are not easily broken. No matter how highly she valued personal freedom,

5. The sailor Zhelezniak (or Zhelezniakov) led the dispersal of the elected Constituent Assembly, which was done on Lenin's orders.

6. Lenin's principal pretext for overthrowing the Provisional Government and seizing power in October, 1917 (November 7, 1917, by the Gregorian Calendar) was to force the election of a Constituent Assembly so as to decide by democratic means who would rule the post-revolutionary Russia. When the Assembly was duly elected in January 1918, it turned out that the Socialist Revolutionaries had won most of the seats and that the Bolshevik deputies were in the minority. Lenin then ordered the Constituent Assembly dispersed by armed sailors led by Zhelezniakov and by a detachment of Latvian sharpshooters who spoke no Russian and were told that the elected socialist and liberal deputies were enemies of the Revolution.

Alexander Kerensky, the leader of the Provisional Government between the February and October Revolutions, was secretly present at the single session of the Constituent Assembly on January 5 and 6, 1918. His account of that experience is to be found in his book *Russia and History's Turning Point* (New York: Duell, Sloan and Pearce, 1965), a selection from which was published in Russian in *The New Review*, no. 84, 1966.

Gippius would always miss Russia. In Warsaw, where the Merezhkovskys ended up right after their flight from Russia, she finished her diary with the following short poem:

> There I love or hate,
> But I understand all of them equally:
> Those who lie and those who are lied to,
> Those who tie the noose
> And those strangled by the noose.
> But here I see no one at all.
> They are all the same. It's all the same.

The Merezhkovskys stayed in Warsaw for nine months and then moved to Paris. They tried in every way to convince Europeans that Bolshevism was a world-wide danger. But no one listened to them. Europe was tired of war, she was resting, she gave parties and didn't want to hear of an armed intervention against the Bolsheviks. Only Germany listened to the Merezhkovskys. She listened and prepared for revenge.

SEVEN

The Last Days of Dmitry Merezhkovsky and Zinaida Gippius

I

Dmitry Merezhkovsky died suddenly in Paris on Sunday, December 7, 1941, the day Japan entered World War II. He was seventy-six. He had not been ill. He was rarely ill. During the last twenty years of his life he had been ill in bed no more than three or four days. He patiently sat out at home unavoidable bouts with the flu, continuing to work. One of the exceptional aspects of his nature was the complete absence of laziness. He would devote only a few hours of each day to writing, always in the morning, and would spend the rest of the day reading and doing research for his next book. Nothing, and certainly no illness, could distract him from his morning work. But at the slightest sign of illness his wife, Zinaida Gippius, would begin to worry, observe him intently with concealed apprehension and not let him out of the house until he recovered. This often led to quarrels between them. Merezhkovsky, feeling better, would be anxious to go for a walk, especially when the weather was good. "To walk is light, not to walk is darkness," he used to say.[1] Gippius, finding he had not

---

1. In Russian, this is a pun on the saying "Learning is light, ignorance is darkness."

quite recovered, would insist that he stay home. Not
wanting to upset her, Merezhkovsky would give in.
They always went for a stroll together. The last year of
his life, she wouldn't let him take so much as a step
without her, not even to the barber. She was afraid something would happen to him.

This constant fear she had for Merezhkovsky seemed
inexplicable, silly, sometimes even ridiculous. But what
could she do? It obsessed her more and more as time
went on. She would have been glad to be rid of it, but
how? "Since my childhood I have been wounded by
death and love," she wrote in her diary. "I am still alive
because love still possesses me and is expressed in fear."
Against the background of world-wide catastrophe, her
fears took on an almost tangible form. "My God! My
God! What will I write in my new green appointment
book?" she asked on the eve of 1941. That was more than
a premonition. It was knowledge. She seemed to know
that Merezhkovsky would die first and that death was
lying in wait for him. But since our times and seasons are
hidden from us, Gippius suffered through every one of
Merezhkovsky's illnesses as though it were the fatal one
and through every day as though it were his last.

> We have happiness, believe me.
> And everyone can share it.
> Our happiness is that suddenly
> We can forget about death.
> Not our falsely audacious reason,
> (Let it know, let it insist),
> But our senses, our blood, our body
> Refuse to remember death.

Poor Zinaida Gippius! A gravestone had weighed her
down since childhood and it stayed there for a lifetime.

To draw even a single breath freely was sometimes happiness. But even that was not always attainable. Everything reminded her of death. "A word, as if between the lines, / The eyes of an ailing baby" and, of course, "Again my blood is poisoned." Even if she were to submit and accept the fact that everything is the will of God, which no one should question, and that everyone is equal before death, how could she forget what was revealed to her and what it was not given to her to forget? But if one cannot "forget the future," why not try to correct it, to alter destiny? And she did make this desperate attempt. She decided that she would be the first of them to leave this world, convinced that even God could not and should not decide otherwise. It seemed to her that there was no better solution for herself and for everyone: "My death—what liberation!" And she seriously began to prepare for it. On January 6, 1922, the Russian Christmas Eve, almost twenty years before Merezhkovsky's death, she broke off the last entry in her diary and placed a large cross in red pencil at the bottom of the page. A month later she wrote in gigantic letters on the next page: "This is the end of all my diaries; henceforth, from a day which is not to come again for more than a century, 2-2-22, begins my 'Concluding Word'."

But this attempt at spiritual suicide, "to extinguish one's soul," as she put it, was not successful. She was still too vital, too full of strength which was fated not to find any application. No matter how hard she tried to destroy herself inwardly, she could not break her will to live. God, in any case, would not change His decision. At the end of "A Concluding Word" she wrote: "No, no, I will rather be enveloped in a fog; it is better to exist 'outside of oneself,' to extinguish one's soul in fact, that is to do it

within oneself as well. Because I cannot go on. I cannot.
It cannot be endured." She did endure, however, despite
her "torture by fear," from which she had nowhere to
hide. But she continued to hope secretly that she would
not see Merezhkovsky's death, that she would depart
first. If God would not change His decision, so much the
worse for Him.

But did Merezhkovsky have a premonition of his own
death? It is difficult to say with certainty. He did not
leave any diaries or letters except for a few business letters. According to Gippius he was ready for death and
accepted it calmly. This is also suggested by his last
poems:

> The sun is setting, the road is ended,
> Night lodging is near, it is time to rest.

Or:

> Soon I will say with a filial smile:
> Welcome, my mother Death.

But whether Merezhkovsky actually foresaw his own
death or only thought about it incidentally as all old
people think about it at times is not important. What is
important is how he felt about it and what he hoped for.
Gippius spoke of death in one of her poems:

> I hate death in any form,
> Only my own, unknown, I love.

Merezhkovsky also loved it, but not because it is "the
heavenly limit to earthly grief," an idea which would not
have been all that original. He loved it as a deliverer
from his double exile, for the eternal joy which it
heralded, the joy of the paradisiac reunion of his earthly
homeland and the one in heaven. For him the thought of

death was inseparable from the thought of Russia. It was not accidental that his last conversation with Gippius on the eve of his death was about Russia. As it was for the ancient Egyptians, death for him was a return to his homeland. In his poem "Drowsiness," which of all his last poems is the only truly prophetic one, without pseudo-foreboding or Nadson-style exclamations, he simply and truthfully describes a sort of vision, the secret meaning of which eludes him, perhaps not entirely accidentally.

> What was it? Morning? Night?
> I don't know where it was.
> . . . .
> Silence, a pathless forest,
> Fields edged with crimson poppies.
> It's all so Russian—a heavenly
> Russian field of ripening rye.
> Lord in Heaven, what does it mean?

he asked, puzzled. But his soul wept with joy, as if it sensed the approaching end of his exile.

The closer the end approached, the more everything otherworldly became for him earthly, native, Russian, and human:

> Lord, I go into the unknown.
> But let it be like my native land.
> Let everything heavenly be for me
> Just the same as it was on earth.

Merezhkovsky might have repeated this prayer, which was written by Gippius. Gippius, by the way, wrote in her diary: "The beyond is closer and more accessible than Russia." As for this world, it appeared to Merezhkovsky to grow ever coarser and more inhuman. Rereading some poems by Khodasevich, he underlined the words "We live in fragile coarseness."[2] This line may have inspired his poem "Most Important":

> Good, evil, insignificant, glorious—
> Perhaps all those are trifles.
> But most important, most important
> Is what frightens me more than the longing for death—
>
> The coarseness of spirit, the coarseness of matter,
> The coarseness of life, of love, of all things.

The triumph of that coarseness, of savagery, of the inhuman in man was war. Merezhkovsky had predicted war long in advance in his book *Secret of the West: Europe-Atlantis,* and the title itself shows what he expected of the war. He began to feel the full weight of his double exile, his double loss, in 1939, at the onset of the catastrophe. Russia had collapsed, but there was the rest of the world. Now the rest of the world was also collapsing. The reign of lies and murder was flourishing luxuriantly in what was once Europe—"the land of holy miracles"[3]—turning it into a hell on earth, in which he was to live out the last two years of his life.

The beginning of the war found the Merezhkovskys in Paris. Fearing air raids, the French government strongly recommended that everyone who could should leave the capital. Their panic was premature. Paris was not threatened with immediate danger. But a week after

2. From Vladislav Khodasevich's poem "It's hardly worth living or singing . . ."

3. From the poem "Reverie" ("Mechta"), written by the Slavophile poet and philosopher Alexei Khomiakov in 1834. The poem laments the imminent decline of Western Europe (called "the land of holy miracles") and predicts that the countries of Eastern Europe will have to take over the West's cultural mission.

the announcement of a general mobilization the Merezh-kovskys left Paris for Biarritz under nightmarish conditions. There they spent three months in relative safety and in December they returned to their Paris apartment.

The winter of 1939–1940 is remembered as the *drôle de guerre*. It was characterized by Boredom with a capital *B*, as Gippius put it. "Oh, how sick and tired I am of the war and the Bolsheviks and everything!" she wrote in her notebook. In January she came down with the flu and didn't go out for two weeks. "I haven't written anything because all I do is lie in bed, thinking about nothing, with the pallid consolation that it is I who am sick, not he." But several days later: "There's nothing wrong with me—and what would it matter? But as for him, he seems to be at it again. He coughs and probably has a fever." "Yes, he's been coughing since morning," she wrote the next day. She began to worry: "No, I can't write. There is such fear in my heart." But by the first of February they had both recovered and resumed their daily strolls.

Every Sunday before their guests arrived (it was a tradition from the old days in St. Petersburg that their friends would gather at their house every Sunday), they would stop by on their walk to see the little Saint Therese of Lisieux in the church dedicated to her on the rue la Fontaine. They loved her dearly and believed that she aided them in difficult moments. In front of her statue in their living room there were always fresh flowers for which they spared no expense. Merezhkovsky was planning to write a book about her and Gippius wrote a number of poems about her. This cult lasted right up to Merezhkovksy's death.

In the spring of 1940 came the events that everyone remembers. The "standstill war" was over. The Germans occupied Norway, Denmark, Holland, and Belgium and invaded France. Paris was threatened. Their friends advised the Merezhkovskys to leave, but they hesitated because they did not have much money. By the beginning of June the pace of events quickened and with great reluctance the Merezhkovskys decided to return to "that vile Biarritz," as Gippius called it. She had reason to dislike it. Fortunately they obtained sleeping car reservations in time and left on Wednesday, June 5, before the general panic began.

Biarritz turned out to be an ordeal. The city was overcrowded. The Hôtel Metropole, where they were staying, was requisitioned several days after their arrival by a government department which had fled from Paris. The Merezhkovskys found themselves out on the street. They found shelter for one night in a suburban villa for which the French writer Georges Duhamel had put down a deposit. He kindly let them stay the night, after which they saw no more of him. The second night they spent in the villa of a woman they knew, where they had stayed during their previous visit. On the third night they found themselves at the Maison Basque, once a decent hotel, but now a flophouse for refugees. There they were stranded for a long time. They didn't even bother looking for more suitable lodgings since they were almost out of money. A room in the Maison Basque was not expensive, only seventy francs a week. If worse came to worse, they could forget about paying—they knew they would not be thrown out.

The Germans entered Paris on June 14. Gippius wrote: "I can hardly go on under the weight of what is happening. Paris occupied by the Germans . . . Am I really writing this?" On June 28 the Germans were in Biarritz. "Oh, what a nightmare," she exclaimed. "Covered with black soot, they popped out of hell in raging numbers, thundering around in vehicles as black and sooty as themselves. It is almost more than I can bear." Her summary of the events of June was terse: "The weather is getting better and better. There are more and more robots with a green sheen. I can bear them less and less. Our situation is growing worse and worse."

The Merezhkovskys' situation was in fact anything but dazzling. Their money was spent. There was no income. In the chaos that life had become, there was no question of advance payments from French publishers. They were cut off from their foreign publishers by the occupation. Friends helped, but they couldn't live on that. There were days when their only food was coffee and stale bread crusts. Poverty, exile, ailments, and old age. Fortunately there was an unknown person, a "good Samaritan," as the Merezhkovskys called him, who brought them food—now cutlets, now porridge, now some berry fool. Those who could afford it would invite them to lunch or dinner. Finally, in order to help them, some friends arranged a celebration in honor of Merezh-kovsky's seventy-fifth birthday under the chairmanship of the French writer Claude Farrère. The celebration was a success and it brought in about seven thousand francs net. The Merezhkovskys left the hateful Maison Basque and moved to a small villa, El Recres, where they settled for the winter.

But about ten days before they moved, Merezhkovsky, after dining at the home of friends somewhere, suc-cumbed to a prolonged and unpleasant, though not dangerous, intestinal ailment from which many people in Biarritz were suffering at the time. Gippius lost her head completely from fear. She thought it was the end. They each had their own room at El Recres, but she moved into Merezhkovsky's room in order to be with him day and night. She could neither think nor write of anything but his health. "It feels good to be at the villa, but he still feels poorly." "He is in pain." "He can no longer go out. He stays in bed all day." "The same, still the same." "He's in pain and nothing helps." Thus it went on for a little over a month until Merezhkovsky went to a good doctor who prescribed the proper medicine. He began to recover slowly and Gippius gradually calmed down. Not for long, however.

They had never lived through a winter like the winter of 1940–1941. It was more and more difficult to breathe in the atmosphere of catastrophe that surrounded them. "My Lady Poverty" was their constant guest. The hunger, the cold—in December the temperature fell to $-18°C$—the constant worries, constant humiliation, and finally illness had all left their mark on Merezhkovsky. Although he was almost as lively and alert as before, at times he looked tired and numb. He was not tired of life which, with all its trivialities, he continued to love like a child; he was tired of what life had become. "This war has aged me," he often repeated. Gippius too was exhausted. The specter of the end pursued her day and night. She tried to banish it, to turn her attention elsewhere, but in vain. Neither detective stories nor little Saint Therese helped.

> I have narrowed it all to one thought,
> I see a single pointed blade.

Even when they learned by chance at the end of August 1940 of the death of their close friend, Dmitry Filosofov, it did not shock her as much as it would have had he died a few months earlier. As for the other misfortunes which fate did not spare them, Gippius reacted to them more or less with indifference. Yes, it was unpleasant and irritating that they were evicted from their Paris apartment for nonpayment of rent and that their furniture was distrained. Many other things were unpleasant, but it was all trivia and could eventually be rectified. The only important thing was for Merezhkovsky to be in good health, avoid irritation, and continue to work.

And work he did, overcoming everything—hunger, cold, illness, and fear. His resistance was truly miraculous. He lost neither his inner freedom nor his clarity of thought. At the Maison Basque, sick and half-starved, he finished the first part of *The Spanish Mystics,* "The Life of Saint John of the Cross," and began the second part, "The Life of Saint Theresa of Avila." At El Recres, having finished with the Spaniards, he immediately began a new book, the last of the cycle *From Jesus to Us*, about little Saint Therese. At the same time he collected material for a book about Goethe. Once he jokingly remarked: "I'm getting good and tired of these saints. Why don't I write about that pagan, Goethe?" But, alas, he was not fated to write about Goethe. He gave a series of public lectures on Leonardo da Vinci and on Pascal. His lecture on the latter elicited furious and ill-informed criticism from orthodox Catholics. A lecture on Napoleon scheduled to take place at the Casino was cancelled at the last minute by the Germans, no one knew why. That was a blow to the Merezhkovskys. They had hoped it would help alleviate their financial problems, since a lecture on this topic would most likely have been a success. And their financial problems were grave indeed. "My Lady Poverty" visited them more and more often and stayed with them longer. Merezhkovsky was able to obtain only one new contract with a publisher—a German one—for his new books. But the conditions were not advantageous and the advance was paltry, to be paid not at once, but in three installments. Merezhkovsky never did see the last two payments.

Early in July 1941 the Merezhkovskys were evicted from El Recres for not paying the rent. They moved into two furnished rooms at the Hermitage Villa where they had spent the second night after their eviction from the Metropole. The landlady extended them credit. There they stayed for about two months. In September they returned at last to Paris to settle their affairs and save their apartment. It was to be their last journey.

They arrived in Paris at 9:00 in the evening on September 9. The number nine positively dogged them. The beginning of their troubles, the beginning of the war was in September, the ninth month, of 1939. Their first departure for Biarritz was on September 9, 1939. They returned to Paris on December 9, 1939. Their return from their second trip to Paris was again on September 9. But Merezhkovsky did not notice the mysterious repetition. He feared the "Devil's dozen," i.e., 13, and Mondays and Fridays. Gippius did not notice either, although she was very attentive to numbers:

> I watch the numbers carefully.
> God gives us numbers as prophetic signs.

Yet it was for Gippius herself that September 9 was always to be a fateful day. It was a lovely late fall in

Paris. The Merezhkovskys were glad to be home in their own apartment, even if it had been distrained by the authorities. Again there were flowers surrounding little St. Therese. Again they would go to visit her on Sundays on the rue la Fontaine. But their salon was empty. Their "Number One Friend" was Victor Mamchenko.[4] Sometimes the Lifar brothers,[5] the Zaitsevs[6] or Tèffi would come by. Ivan Bunin was not in Paris. He was in the south, in Grasse. But a new disciple of Merezhkovsky's appeared, Nicholas Zhuravlev, a medical student who wrote poetry in French. Once or twice the distinguished, white-bearded old sage, Teslenko, a onetime member of the Duma, dropped by. His fate coincided strangely with Merezhkovsky's last days, as did the fate of their old friend from Russia, Prince Vladimir Argutinsky.[7]

Life returned to its normal course, as if Biarritz had never happened. Merezhkovsky worked, rested, and went for walks. In the evening Gippius would read detective novels by the score in her "green corner." Food, however, was a problem. They weren't in the habit of buying on the black market where everything was available in abundance, nor could they afford it. At one time in Soviet Russia twenty-two years earlier, Gippius was still able to write such humorous poems as:

4. Victor Mamchenko, a prolific émigré poet of some originality, who often acted as a good Samaritan for the older exiled Russian writers, such as Remizov and Gippius.

5. Serge Lifar, the premier danseur and choreographer of the Paris Opera, and his brother Leonid.

6. The novelist and author of literary biographies Boris Zaitsev and his wife Vera.

7. A friend and correspondent of Anton Chekhov in his youth, Prince Vladimir Argutinsky-Dolgorukov was an art expert, closely associated with Sergei Diaghilev.

> No need for either milk or chocolate,
> No need for candy, salt, and suchlike hoards.
> My need for heat has also disappeared of late,
> Since the Committee for the Poor shall give me
> Two pairs of wooden boards.

Now things were different. Now their very lives depended on the availability of "milk or chocolate." More than anything else they feared the cold. Winter was approaching and there was no coal. In October Merezhkovsky began to freeze. He worked in a warm overcoat with a rug over his legs. Cigarettes were now beyond their means. The Merezhkovskys missed them terribly. But they had gone through this already in the past. Once, when they were walking through the Tauride Gardens after the Revolution, Gippius composed this four-line poem extemporaneously:

> Lowering my eyelids with indifference
> (It has become a steady habit),
> I light a golden cigarette
> With a precious silver match.

Everything was repeating itself. The past was becoming visible through the present like a corpse through a half-rotten shroud. Everything that was happening in the world then was only a repetition on a gigantic scale of what had happened in Russia. All the same, Merezhkovsky did not turn his back on Russia. He believed in her no matter what.

October and November passed, and December came. Merezhkovsky finished the first part of *Little Therese* and was writing the second. He no longer worked in his own room, but in the living room where it was warmer. Gippius, sunk in her own joyless thoughts, would sit in a chair near him, sewing something. Every now and then he would read her a passage that seemed particularly successful. "Is it good?" he would ask. Gippius did not always approve. If she said it was bad, Merezhkovsky would be crushed. He would argue and grow angry. The next day or that same evening, however, he would rewrite what she had rejected and it would indeed emerge improved.

At the end of the month preceding his death, on Saturday, November 29, Gippius's diary suddenly broke off, as if she sensed approaching disaster and fell mute from terror. That first week in December they went to visit St. Therese two days earlier than usual, on Friday, December 5, again as if they sensed that Sunday would be too late. On Saturday, after a short walk and a rest in a café, the Merezhkovskys returned home and had dinner. Merezhkovsky put on his coat, took a book and settled down on the sofa in the living room in the "green corner." His head ached a little and his hands were chilled, but one doesn't, after all, read with gloves on. Gippius was next to him, writing something at the table. Evening tea. A conversation about Russia. Gippius did not yield her position: above and beyond Russia there is freedom. Merezhkovsky did not disagree. "Yes, yes, but that is too abstract. Without Russia freedom is not sweet." "For me it is," Gippius said angrily.

Around 1:00 A.M. he went to his room. He had a habit of turning off the light in the dining room and smoking his last cigarette on the sofa there before going to bed. "What are you doing there in the dark?" Gippius had once asked him. "I'm searching for hope." But that night he didn't smoke his cigarette, and when Gippius asked him "What about your 'cigarette of hope'?" he answered, "It doesn't matter. Next time." He went to bed and Gippius came in to say goodnight. "You and I love differently," he continued their talk about Russia. "I'm like Blok: 'But even as you are, my Russia, you are the most precious of all countries to me.'[8] You don't understand that," he added. "But it doesn't matter."

On Sunday, December 7, Merezhkovsky got up, as always, around eight o'clock. He switched the electric heater and the light in the bathroom on. He took his teacup with its leftover tea into the dining room, put a handkerchief, a brush, and a comb on the mantle and sat down in the wicker chair by the stove. Here, after washing, he would comb his hair and in the meantime warm his hands. But the stove had gone out. He started to put in a little more coal.

At 8:30 the French cleaning woman arrived. She made coffee and brushed clothes. Coming down the corridor, she looked through the glass doors into the dining room which she intended to tidy up a bit while Merezhkovsky was washing. She was astonished that Merezhkovsky had been sitting by the stove so long that morning. She didn't notice anything except that he seemed pale. Finally, at 9:00, she became alarmed and went into the room. She found Merezhkovsky unconscious in the chair. She rushed to Gippius's bedroom, flung back the window curtains, and woke her: "Venez vite, monsieur est malade." Gippius, who usually took a long time to wake up, was instantly on her feet: "Oui, je viens, je viens." There it was, the very thing she had feared so much, a morning so much like that morning in St. Petersburg

8. From an untitled poem by Alexander Blok that begins: "To sin shamelessly, without respite . . ."

long ago when her mother had died and her beloved Nanny Dasha had awakened her with the same urgency: "Hurry, hurry, Mama isn't well."

Throwing on a warm quilted robe, Gippius ran to the dining room and went up to him: "What's the matter, dear? Are you ill?" Merezhkovsky didn't answer. She brought some cologne and rubbed his face with it. The cleaning woman went down to the concierge who telephoned the doctor. He arrived in fifteen minutes. They carried Merezhkovsky into his room and put him in bed. The doctor gave him a camphor injection and put a cold compress on his head and another on his chest. Merezhkovsky's breathing was accelerated. Gippius stood in her black robe with her back to him, facing the icons. Her lips were whispering something. The doctor gave him another injection and left, promising to return before lunch. There was no hope: he was hemorrhaging in the brain. Half an hour after the doctor left, Merezhkovsky died without regaining consciousness.

Gippius left his room. She was very pale, but outwardly calm. The manuscript of Merezhkovsky's book about little Therese was on the desk in the living room where everything had been prepared for his morning's work. It ended abruptly on page thirteen:

> Little Therese is extraordinary because she is so very ordinary. She wraps herself up in drab conventionality like the pitiful worm that hides itself in a drab cocoon, the worm of which the True Son of God, the Creator of worlds and of eternity, speaks through the lips of King David: "But I am a worm, and no man; a reproach of men and despised of the people." (Psalms 22:6). The pitiful worm wraps itself in a dark cocoon so that it may fly out as a resurrected butterfly, dazzling white like the sun.

That Sunday, December 7, was endless. The Merezhkovskys' apartment had been full of people since morning. Many of them came for a Sunday visit, knowing
nothing of Merezhkovsky's death. One of those innocent
visitors was Teslenko. Gippius sat in the half-lighted living room surrounded by women. Teslenko sat down in
the dining room. No one paid him any attention. Leonid
Lifar was writing something at the edge of the table.
Suddenly Teslenko asked him: "Why isn't Dmitry
Sergeyevich coming out today? Isn't he well?" (When
Gippius went to church exactly one year later for a req-
uiem for Merezhkovsky, the first thing she saw was a
casket standing in the middle of the church. Teslenko's
funeral was to be the next day.) The news of Merezhkovsky's death spread quickly through Paris, and the
next day, Monday, almost all their friends attended the
memorial service read by the Merezhkovskys' young
nephew, Father Dmitry Klepinin. Among them was
Prince Vladimir Argutinsky. But he did not enter the
room where Merezhkovsky was lying in state. He stayed
alone in the dining room because he was afraid of corpses.
The funeral took place on Wednesday morning at the
church on rue Daru. He was buried in the Russian cem-
etery of Saint Geneviève de Bois. Before the service,
Tatiana Manukhina, the wife of the doctor, went up to
Gippius and whispered to her that Tuesday evening
Argutinksy had suddenly died.

II

Zinaida Gippius without Dmitry Merezhkovsky
. . . It was almost as impossible to imagine as Merezhkovsky without Gippius. Only death could have sep-

arated them. In human terms it was cruel, but perhaps in God's terms it was merciful that he died first, quickly and without suffering. What would it have been like for Gippius if he were to have died slowly, of a painful illness? What would it have done to him if he had had to live through her final agony? But she reacted to the blow in human terms, not in God's terms, taking it as if it were an undeserved hurt. It even seemed to her that her spirit had died. "I am writing this now when *my* life is over. I sense and know it," she wrote ten months later. "I am still alive only physically and therefore others do not see and cannot understand my death." But hadn't she literally said the same thing twenty-two years earlier: "My life is over"? True, she said, "I knew everything and nothing. Only now, having suffered the final thing in life, I actually know something. That is, only when that which was my life had ended." But was it really over? The death of someone near and dear may leave an invisible scar on the soul, an internal wound, but it doesn't kill the soul. Only sin kills the soul. No, the real tragedy of Gippius was that in spite of the blow she had suffered she was still alive and that her inextinguishable life force could no longer find an outlet. There was much that she still could do—she had by no means said her last word. But in a world that had become empty for her since Merezhkovsky's death there was nothing and no one she could count on for support. And the current state of the world made her feel nothing but boredom and nausea— that special nausea that exists only in hell and for which there isn't even a word in any human language:

> For subterranean and endless nausea
> There are no earthly words, for words are not enough.

She withdrew into herself and she even contemplated suicide. "It is only what is left of my religion," she admitted, "(yes, what is left, alas! My insignificance basically could not hold out against the blow it sustained) that keeps me from leaving life of my own accord (or is it my weak will?). But I have nothing to live *on* or *for*." What an admission! But wouldn't it have been more true, closer to reality had she said: "It's not that *I* want to kill myself. I am *being* killed." Everything was killing her, everything was against her—people, God. Life itself seemed to reject her. She could not forgive God for Merezhkovsky's death. Little Therese was in disgrace under a black cover and with no flowers in front of her. Gippius no longer went to visit her on the rue La Fontaine and would never go again. Her rebellion, however, was very much like that of a helpless child. In the face of death she was as defenseless as a small child whom someone had hurt for no known reason:

> I don't know, I don't know, and I don't want to know.
> I only suffer and I remain silent.

She felt cold and lonely. For her the world was like an icy desert where she froze, like Kay in Andersen's fairy tale "The Snow Queen":

> How this frost wearies me,
> This freezing within my heart.
> I would cry so my heart would melt,
> But I have no tears.

It would melt, but not before the sharp icicles formed a word which she forgot and could not remember: eternity.

She was seventy-two years old but she still looked youthful and elegant in her black dress. As always, she devoted a great deal of time to her appearance. She began to go out, receive guests, and little by little she began to work. She wanted to write a book about Merezhkovsky because she alone knew and remembered everything about him. She felt pressed for time—she knew she did not have long to live. She also wrote poetry—an inordinately long poem, "The Last Circle," which she re-worked endlessly. But that was her outward, "daytime" appearance. She hid her suffering. It was secret, dark, and avid like a strange monster that fed on her blood. At night she had constant nightmares. She would often jump up in her sleep, repeating, "Oui, je viens, je viens." Gliding into the dining room like a ghost, she would go up to the stove and lean over the empty chair where Merezhkovsky had been sitting that morning and say the same words: "What's the matter, dear? Are you ill?" If anyone pulled back the window curtains in her room too quickly in the morning, the sound would make her relive everything and she would hurriedly jump up, getting tangled in the blankets, and again repeat, "Oui, je viens, je viens." This went on for many months.

When her sister Anna died suddenly in the street on November 11, 1942, she wrote in her diary: "Since that day in November when Asya died, every hour I feel more and more cut off from the flesh of the world (from Mother)." But that tie with "the flesh of the world," with Mother Earth, was not yet broken and perhaps would never break completely.

I love the whole of you, my Only One.
The whole of you is mine!

> Together we'll be resurrected beyond a mysterious bound-
> ary,
> Together—both you and I,

she said in her poem about the earth. There still flickered
in her heart the hope for a miracle. That miracle was so
simple, so possible. "The little person with a large
grief," as Gippius was called in her childhood, waited for
her mother to soothe and calm her. That was all. "I don't
understand my death, or perhaps I don't fear it. I have to
exist within the tangible love of someone else." But that
miracle which might have melted her heart did not happen. Around her was the same icy expanse; the same cold
was within her:

> As if a sharp-edged piece of ice
> Were secretly placed in me instead of a heart.

Shortly before her death a cry escaped her: "But I
don't care now. I only want to leave, to leave, not to
hear, not to see, to forget." And little by little she did
leave, almost imperceptibly, going toward that miracle
she had searched for and waited for her whole life.

She did a great deal of work at night as was her habit,
smoking innumerable cigarettes. She was in a hurry to
finish her book on Merezhkovsky. When she was too
tired to write she turned to sewing and mending her
linen until her work slipped from her hands from exhaus-
tion. Then, finally, she would go to bed almost at dawn.
She got up early. This seriously affected her health. First
her left leg swelled up. Her personal physician did not
think it serious and prescribed an ointment. But one
Sunday at the end of March, 1944, while she was sitting
in her room reading, she suddenly announced with com-

plete calm: "I think I am becoming paralyzed." She complained of a prickly sensation and that the right side of her body felt numb. She was told not to worry. However, the French physician, Doctor André, who had been called on Monday morning, found the situation serious: sclerosis of the brain, where several areas had been affected. This of course was concealed from Gippius. She thought that her arm ached and was numb because of poor circulation caused by constricted blood vessels, especially since the tips of her fingers had been known to go numb in the past. Moreover, during his last year Merezhkovsky used to lean so heavily on her arm during their strolls that it was no wonder her arm was tired. "I literally carried him," she told the doctor. "But I do not regret it."

Several days passed. Gippius tried to continue to work, to type a new version of her interminable narrative poem. But the pain in her arm and her body grew worse and she became discouraged. She gave up everything, including reading, and spent entire days lying on the couch without moving at all. She was well cared for and ate well. She lacked for nothing. And little by little she began to recover. After two months she could not only go out but could even write, and if she refrained from writing, it was only because she was waiting for her arm to mend completely. In the summer her condition had improved to such an extent that in August, after the liberation of Paris by the Allies, she went on foot to the Eiffel Tower to buy cigarettes on the American black market. After wandering around in the crowd for about an hour she returned home again on foot.

The fall and beginning of the winter of 1945 passed and brought no major changes. She was now a little worse, now a little better. For a time she was bothered by pains in the left side of her head. But they went away. She began to write a little, only short letters, because she didn't want to tire her arm. She was favoring it in order to be able to write her book on Merezhkovsky. She was a masterful letter writer and was famous for her epistolary art. Her handwriting had hardly changed. It became perhaps a little less sure and a little smaller, but that must have been because she was out of practice.

No other changes were noticeable in her. As always, she was true to herself, did not give up her views and held steadfastly to them. She did not submit to God or Saint Therese. If her illness at times brought out some of her bad qualities too sharply, she knew how to soften them and restore her equilibrium. She did have her share of bad traits and she herself clearly saw what she called the obverse side of her own character. Not for nothing did she frequently qualify herself as a "nonentity," "a good-for-nothing" or as "empty-headed" and she would resolve to do better. There was in her not only a "little girl lost," not only a little Saint Therese, so frozen and abandoned by God that it was almost impossible to look at her without tears, but also a witch, known only to those few friends who had remained loyal to her. But those few did know her well enough. Loyalty, incidentally, was what she valued above all else, and she herself was always loyal:

> I do not want to claim the credit,
> But I have never betrayed love,
> And I have never been unfaithful
> To it or a woman or a friend.

And for this she will certainly be given credit.

Merezhkovsky, for all his brusque manner and his sometimes astonishing impracticality, was wise and meek. Gippius was natively intelligent but there wasn't a drop of wisdom in her. And as for meekness, what meekness does a witch have? One distinguished dignitary of the Church, a member of the St. Petersburg Religious-Philosophical Society (which was initially conceived by Gippius), always referred to her as the "white she-devil." There was, of course, nothing even remotely diabolical about her, but at times a supernatural power, similar to the one that possessed Turgenev's Klara Milich,[9] took hold of her.

Strange and terrifying as it may seem, doesn't that almost saintly half-witch, half-vampire have something indefinable in common with Gippius? In any case, Gippius, like Klara, takes one away from this life:

> Forgive me for all those
> Whom I took away from this life.
> Took away from sleep and from peace,
> Away from wives and from mothers.

The only difference is that Klara "took away" for herself, while Gippius did not. At least that was what she maintained. But how can one in deeds and not in words separate what is heavenly from what is earthly in love, separate the holy from the sinful, and higher interests from personal gain? And did Gippius ever succeed in separating completely in her soul—and that is the whole point—Saint Therese from Klara, the freezing child

9. The heroine of Ivan Turgenev's mystical novella "Klara Milich," a young actress who commits suicide after being spurned by the man with whom she fell in love, and then forces him from beyond the grave to reciprocate her love.

from the enamored witch? For all her purity and saintliness, Saint Therese came within a hair's breadth of perdition. Klara, in spite of her destructive passion, came within a hair's breadth of salvation. They mutually cancel each other out. But perdition and salvation was for them the same. The impossibility of separating them completely in her life and the duality and confusion of her life because of it was what caused Gippius constant torment. "My life (isn't it the life of the world?) is only a chalice in the hand of the Lord, and in it there seethes wine full of confusion." This says everything.

The days flew past. Nothing happened, that is, nothing definite. Gippius, half-reclining on her couch which was now placed by the table in the dining room—the only warm room in her apartment—was rereading *Contemporary Annals*[10] out of boredom. But she had a new distraction, a cat. Not Siamese, but an ordinary gray tabby. Victor Mamchenko, her "Number One Friend" once brought her a tiny, frightened kitten from Meudon. It grew up and, although Gippius didn't like cats, she became attached to this one. The cat hardly ever left her lap. It was warm and soft. And alive. If it was stubborn and didn't come to her, Gippius would try to lure it: "You're a cat. You're a nice cat. Come here now, come." At first the cat would not cooperate, wanting to show its independence. Finally it would come, acting as if it all had happened by chance.

In the middle of March Gippius did something highly imprudent which accelerated the progress of her illness. She went to the hairdresser's to have her hair washed.

10. *Sovremennye zapiski*, one of the finest Russian literary journals of all time, which was published in Paris from 1920 to 1940.

But that was only a pretext. The secret reason for going was to get a permanent wave. Under no circumstances did she ever stop being concerned about her appearance.[11] In one of her old parodies, in which she spared no one, not even herself, she had a "Shady Lady," representing herself, utter a phrase that became a classic in the Merezhkovskys' circle: "On the day Pompeii was destroyed / I curled my hair with curling papers." In fact, she usually had her hair done on the anniversary of her mother's death and on that of Merezhkovsky's. She would have consented, it seems, even to having a permanent done in her grave. It was a lifesaving habit which helped her to endure and not lose her spirits in those moments when will power alone would not have been enough. Even when she no longer had any idea of what was going on around her, she still would massage her face every night with *lait de beauté* before going to bed and would try to do her hair without outside help. She imagined herself after death as still being alive. "When I die," she said a few weeks before her death, "please put a little makeup on my face." Her incredible, vital strength was the only kind she possessed, not only in her soul, but in her body as well, as she herself admitted. In spite of her fragility and delicacy, her hothouse airs, she was

11. On Zinaida Gippius's concern with her clothes and appearance at the end of her life and also on Vladimir Zlobin's role as her cook, houseboy, and all-around factotum during that period, see Nina Berberova, *The Italics Are Mine* (New York: Harcourt, Brace and World, 1969), p. 243ff. Zlobin's selfless devotion to Gippius and the highhanded, inconsiderate treatment to which she could on occasion subject him are strikingly illustrated in the recollections of Greta Gerell, as cited by Temira Pachmuss (*Zinaida Hippius: An Intellectual Profile*, pp. 399, 400, and 402).

physically strong, much stronger and more hardy than Merezhkovsky had been. Her blood pressure was like a seventeen-year-old's and her heart and lungs were healthy. Anyone else in her place would not have survived even for a year.

She returned from the hairdresser in the best of spirits. But the results of her permanent soon became apparent. The dry heat of the electric current affected the blood vessels in her brain. In two days her condition became considerably worse. The thick volume of *Contemporary Annals* which she was reading on the couch after dinner fell from her hands. What was happening? Why? It was such a chore to move her arm. And her leg was dragging. She was perplexed. Everything was quite in order. What could be the matter? Doctor André, who was called the next day, found that the brain areas that coordinate movement had been affected. Gippius was reassured as if she were a child—it's nothing, it will pass. But the doctor was alarmed. The illness had taken a dangerous turn.

Nevertheless, she again improved. But she was no longer the same, the illness was devouring her. There could be no question of writing, given the condition of her arm. She could move only from room to room and even that with difficulty. Her stroll to the hairdresser's was her last outing. Her nearsightedness and deafness grew worse. But she did continue to read without glasses, as she had always done. She refused to wear glasses out of sheer coquetry. From time to time friends came to see her. She would greet them politely, but their conversation bored her. She seemed absent and her answers showed that she had not been listening. She was no longer interested in anyone or anything. She spent whole days on the couch in the dining room with a book and her inseparable cat which didn't leave her for a moment.

Thus slowly drooping and growing colder
Do we draw closer to our beginnings.

In the first few days of August she was again worse. "The descent downhill is not too bad." Actually, it was very bad. But she didn't understand, didn't realize that it was a descent toward the end. The worse it became, the greater was her astonishment as she asked: "What is it? Why is this happening?" Only once did she express a fleeting doubt: "Could this be the end?" But no, that's unbelievable. On June 7, three months before she died, she managed to scratch out with her left hand several lines in her diary, which were her last: "I am sick and I won't recover. But I'm still not dying and maybe I won't die for a long time." Although she neither saw nor understood her death ("I will die and never see her eyes"), her soul was preparing for it, knowing how terrible it is to fall into "the hands of the living God." And Zinaida Gippius, that proud person, submitted. In March 1945, she wrote, "Outwardly, everything is bad (for me). Everything. But perhaps in terms of God it isn't bad—how can one know? I am in pain, in pain in every way, but maybe that is just what I deserve." She ended her last entry on June 7 with the words "I deserve very little." And she added: "How wise and just God is."

In the last week of August she began to have trouble speaking. "What is happening to me?" she asked in unceasing amazement. "I want to speak and I can't." She thought that she was not being given proper treatment and that it was all the fault of the doctor who was temporarily replacing Doctor André. One morning she woke up and wanted to say something but could manage only a few incoherent words. That night she lost consciousness for a few minutes and almost stopped breathing. When she came to, her ability to speak had suddenly returned. "My last thought before I lost consciousness," she said, "was: thank God. It's the end. And my first thought when I came to was: what a bore! I have to begin all over again." But it was only a short respite, followed by a headlong descent.

After Friday, August 31, she not only lost her coherence of speech but could hardly swallow. Nevertheless, at lunch (she was still brought to the table) she heartily drank a cup of boullion and managed to get down half a beef patty, mashed potatoes, apple sauce and coffee. She smoked a cigarette, not forgetting to return the holder to the round box next to her plate. Then she rested. But by evening she could, alas, no longer say a word or swallow a drop. Doctor André came almost straight from the train station. "Pauvre madame!" he said. But she could neither hear nor recognize him. He prescribed injections of physiological saline twice a day and camphor.

On the evening of Saturday, September 1, Father Vasily Zenkovsky gave her communion. She sat listlessly at the table in the dining room, understanding nothing. But she did swallow the wafer. On Sunday she was moved from the living room to her bedroom. Her faithful cat followed. She was happy in that small but sunny room with a window overlooking the spacious courtyard of the Catholic school of Saint Jean de Passy. Through the window you could see the sky and the tops of the trees as yet untouched by fall. There was silence and emptiness all around. Anything not needed had been removed. Only a bed, a couch, a dresser with a few bare necessities, a table, and a wicker chair remained in the room. She lay facing the window under an icon of the Mother of God. When the sun shone into the room the shutters were partly closed. The sun made the room warm. Did she feel the warmth, that last caress?

> Will her thin, transparent crown,
> The autumnal green of her eyes,
> Flash upon me for the last time?

She lay motionless, raised high upon the pillows. Now and then she moaned quietly. With her good hand she would grasp like a child at whatever was there, at the blanket, a towel, a spoon used to pour grape juice with lemon down her throat so it wouldn't be so tormentingly parched. She lost her ability to hear, see, speak, or think—she had forgotten how. She was like a sick little girl—Therese or Klara—what did it matter which? The doctor gave assurances that she wasn't suffering. But she looked more and more frightful with every passing hour.

It was as if time had stopped in the room. Every moment was an eternity. But time was also flying with vertiginous speed. The same precipitous immobility and tautness was there in her barely living body. No, the doctor was wrong: she was suffering. But the suffering was not in her, she was in it. It covered her, penetrated her through and through, carried her with precipitous immobility into the unknown, like a fiery stream amid eternal ice in which her soul was purified and revived.

> To go, if only to the threshold.
> Ages and ages . . . No more strength.
> Then someone strong, and yet not stern
> Caused me to stop my frightful journey.

It was a quiet, gentle morning followed by an equally quiet, pale sunlit day. Gippius sat in bed, breathing with difficulty. Suddenly her lifeless, unseeing eyes were lit up by something, by a kind of radiance. She looked around herself, as if by some miracle she had become her old self again. She could neither say a word nor move, but she spoke with her eyes. In her glance there shone a boundless tenderness, boundless gratitude. Two tears flowed down her cheeks. That was when, at last, her heart finally thawed. One more look and then she closed her eyes and died. Her face became wondrously beautiful. On it there was an expression of the most profound happiness.

> And you will come to me in that unique hour,
> And cover me with the dark wings of happiness.

That hour came at 3:33 P.M. The day was Sunday, September 9, 1945.

Index

Designer:	Wolfgang Lederer
Compositor:	Interactive Composition Corp.
Printer:	Thomson-Shore, Inc.
Binder:	Thomson-Shore, Inc.
Text:	VIP Garamond
Display:	VIP Trump Medieval
Cloth:	Joanna Arrestox B 34620
Paper:	60 lbs. P&S offset laid, B-32